THE WOUNDED

TELLING OUR STORIES

TELLING OUR STORIES

WRESTLING WITH A FRESH LANGUAGE
FOR THE SPIRITUAL JOURNEY

Alison Leonard

DARTON · LONGMAN + TODD

First published 1995 by
Darton, Longman and Todd Ltd
1 Spencer Court
140–142 Wandsworth High Street
London SW18 4JJ

ISBN 0–232–52097–6

A catalogue record for this book is available
from the British Library

Phototypeset by Intype, London
Printed and bound in Great Britain
by Redwood Books, Trowbridge

In memory of
George Gorman,
who first trusted me to speak

CONTENTS

Foreword   ix
Acknowledgements   xi

1 *Introduction*   1
  Spiritual/religious   1
  Language as discovery   3
  Belief and experience   5
  Where I come from   9
  Paradox and risk   10

2 *Let me be warmed*   15
  Original impotence   16
  Eternity and rules   20
  The power of the absent   24

Interval – *A Day in the Life of an Unbeliever*   30

3 *The girl in the bathroom singing*   38
  Religion versus sex   40
  Conversion   44
  Outside Christianity   48

4 *Discovering my own heartbeat*   51
  Did God care for me?   53
  Israel – holy, holy and differently holy   58
  Power   60
  Belief structures and personal perception   62

Interval – *Meditation on a Meditation*   66

5 *Drawing a profile for that which has no form*   72
   Silence   74
   Revelations   76
   Reclaiming my journey, recognising the Other   82

6 *First and last mysteries*   85
   Ecstatic religious experience   88
   Writing: the mystery of creativity   89
   Sex . . .   92
   . . . and sexuality   95
   . . . and sensuality, and pain   97

Interval – *On Shadows*   102

7 *Healings and leadings*   110
   Openness to suffering   113
   God's will, or the right way   115
   Forgiveness   119
   Building a spiritual community   121

8 *Transforming me into us*   124
   Making decisions   125
   Ritual   127
   Partnership, and the transition of birth   129
   Death and its rituals   132
   Tension and paradox   135

Postscript – *Entering my journey, offering our stories* 137
   Alone   137
   Together   139
   The pattern   142
   The circle   143

References   146

Index   151

FOREWORD

The 'Wounded Pilgrim' series is inspired by the belief that spiritual growth demands an openness to experience and a willingness to accept the challenge of self-knowledge despite the suffering, confusion and agony of spirit which this can involve.

Each author in the series has agreed to take the risk of exposing his or her vulnerability and inner struggle so that others may find comfort and support as they, too, seek the courage to continue on their own spiritual pilgrimage. The books are offered as nourishment for the many seekers in our society who yearn for understanding and encouragement but have all too often experienced the bewilderment and even the hostility of their co-religionists in the institutional Churches. The series responds to the call for a decade of evangelism or evangelization, but does so out of the pain and woundedness which inevitably accompany the determination to be true to experience. There is no spirit of crusading or triumphalism to be found in these pages. Instead, there is the paradoxically fragile resilience of those who have not allowed their fear to prevent them entering the eye of the storm.

Alison Leonard is a professional writer and so it is not surprising that her struggle revolves around the use of language. Words are powerful. In my own work as a counsellor I know only too well the pain and suffering which can result from the false labelling of experience, or from the very absence of an adequate language to describe both the ecstatic and the dark aspects of human existence. Words can give life, but they can also systematically poison the spirit. Sometimes, too, they imprison us in a cage of the mind so that we dare not risk the flights of imagination which could set us free to defy convention or refute those who have the audacity to define our life's pilgrimage for us.

As she courageously invites her readers into dialogue and reveals the cost of her own gradual refusal to collude with a language that does not belong to her, Alison throws down a gauntlet. She demands that we come clean with ourselves and face the possibility that we, too, may often speak a borrowed language behind which we seek protection from the painful quest which is inevitable if we commit ourselves to the promptings of the Spirit which promises – and threatens – to lead us into all truth. This is a strong if gentle challenge, for it points to a freedom which humankind is loath to embrace. Most of us most of the time prefer to be told what to believe and what to do, even if the message is as vapid as the television advertisement telling us to buy something we neither need nor want.

This is a book about language, and yet it may turn you upside down because it does not flinch from entering some of those areas of experience where customarily only poets, novelists and mystics dare to tread. Alison invites us to take the risk of discovering that we, too, can fashion our own unique language to describe what it means to be human and to be full of divine promise. At the same time she challenges us to listen to each other, and to celebrate the complex harmonies of the music we shall hear when we find our own voices to express what previously we had scarcely dared to think or to feel. Perhaps, too, we shall then know something of the music of the spheres and recognise the passionately vibrant silence of the Garden in the cool of the day. Certainly we shall know more than a thing or two about what it means to be fully human and only a tiny bit lower than the angels.

BRIAN THORNE
Norwich, 1995

ACKNOWLEDGEMENTS

I'd like to thank Frank Sharman, Abigail King and Clare Willott
for their constant support; Gil Skidmore for discussions on spiritual
autobiography; Eric Maddern for discussions on ritual and the
metaphor of the story-telling circle in the final chapter; Ben Pink
Dandelion of the *God and Sex Project* (GASP) for clarification of
concepts of sexual and spiritual energy in Chapter 6; Rev. Alfred
Willetts for the quotation at the beginning of Chapter 1; Adam
Curle and Ruth Fawell for many years of loving correspondence
on these issues; Neil Rhodes for his insights; and Anna Sharman,
Cathy Sharman, Elizabeth Cave and other members of the *Quaker
Faith and Practice* group, f/Friends at Chester Quaker Meeting and
other Wirral and North Wales Meetings, Elisabeth Salisbury, Elin
Robson, Dr Daphne Hampson, Margaret McNeil, Ieman Hassan,
Jen Darling, Patrick Jones, Mary Johnson, Maia and Serena and
the others, Lucy Goodison, Sameena Saeed, Jean Ure, Oliver Post-
gate, Anne Hosking, Gillian Lewitt, Sarah Gornall, Joan Bowers,
Jane Martin, Pete Owen, Ros Morley, Patricia Pulham, members
of the Quaker Women's Group through their publications, Ella
Speirs, Rose Flint, Murray Watts, Sarah Taylor, Lila Towle, Sue
Parkinson, Angela Burton, and countless other friends, colleagues
and relations for listening patiently and feeding back ideas. And
for permission to quote: H. A. Williams, Brian Patten, Joan
Benner, Ann Oakley, Brian Keenan, Shirley Lady Anglesey
(daughter of Charles Morgan), Anne Wade, Jackie Kohnstamm,
Canon W. H. Vanstone, John Berger, Sheila Rowbotham, Penelope Farmer and Michèle Roberts. And Mary-Jean Pritchard and
Jane Williams of Darton, Longman and Todd for having faith in
the book at its inception and as it progressed, and finally Brian
Thorne, editor of the 'Wounded Pilgrim' series, for his support,

advice, challenge and, in the literal sense of the word, encouragement.

ALISON LEONARD

1

INTRODUCTION

Listen, Pilgrim! There are no roads.
Roads are made by walking.

*(Sign above Richard Rohr's cabin
in Albuquerque, New Mexico)*

This book is a personal spiritual journey conducted through the medium of language. I am a writer, and I'm fascinated by language. Not only are human ideas conveyed in language, they are actually formed by the language available to us. In a religious context, our Western Christian ideas – even our feelings – are moulded by words like 'Lord', 'sin', 'redemption', 'Zion', and phrases such as 'the house of David', 'the lions' den', 'the power and the glory', 'Onward Christian Soldiers'. All spiritual journeys – those that have been recorded – are passed on to us through a particular type of language. When Emperor Julian the Apostate wrote, *'Vicisti, Galilaee'* ('You have conquered, Galilean'), he was expressing religious belief through the language of warfare; when Thomas Merton wrote heart-rendingly about his orphaned state he asked: 'When wind and winter turn our vineyard/to a bitter Calvary,/ what hands come out and crucify us?'[1]

I have found that, if I'm to be true to myself, these are not my words. But what *are* my words?

Spiritual/religious

I have written, 'This book is a personal *spiritual* journey'. Why do I write 'spiritual' rather than 'religious'? Because the word 'religious', for me, means 'church', and 'church' means 'traditional God-language'. I find Christian language too loaded with historical baggage to be helpful. Growing up as a girl in the church, I felt excluded. Later, I found myself amongst people who had been

1

wounded by Christian attitudes and concepts, or were exasperated beyond enduring by the tortoise pace of change. I gained an increasing number of friends who, like myself, were spiritual seekers exhausted by Christian patriarchy, and had found that their sexual or other personal experience made them feel that the people of the Bible made no place for them. We all grew up within the Christian tradition, but it failed to nurture us. Its language no longer spoke for us.

Let me try to unpack my meaning when I use the word 'spiritual'. For me, the spiritual journey is a search for meaning: for a deeper, broader awareness of my existence than the material or even the emotional or the psychological can give. It is a search for truth: the truth for myself, *of* myself, and the truth for others, and then the search for links between those different glimpses. It is a search for love, for ways to become a more loving person and develop the kind of loving community that might give a foretaste of lives beyond this one. Each moment is part of a lifelong quest. If a day seems not to have any spiritual aspect to it at all, I can be sure that a spiritual bombshell is just round the corner. I realise that I can be accused of using the word 'spiritual' to apply simply to things that appeal to me, merely to things that 'feel good'. But things spiritual sometimes feel extremely bad: unaccountable, disturbing, leading into dark nights, sucking me down into tunnels of despair. George Fox, the first Quaker, found that there was an 'ocean of darkness and death' as well as the 'infinite ocean of light and love'.[2] In fact, to divide the spiritual from the non-spiritual works against its essence. The spiritual is wholeness.

If we see our lives as a spiritual journey, the question must be: why do we see it this way? There seems no need, in this rational and technological age, for the notion that we are spiritual beings. We could just get on with earning a living and rearing our families, plus, if we've any time left over, struggle for the betterment of humanity. Those of us who adopt the concept of 'spirituality' are no finer people than those who don't. We aren't necessarily any happier.

But the quest for the spiritual – the interpretation of life as spiritual – seems a necessity, almost a compulsion. Some of us hold vital beliefs about the nature of life and the place of God in it. Others feel a sense of mystery that no material or logical explanation can dispel. For yet others there persists a moral quest for which spirituality is the only philosophical base. For me it's some of each of these, but I tend to describe it in much more basic and everyday terms. I feel an impulse, amounting to a longing, to put the small events and tiny processes of my life into a larger and more creative context. I need to make connections. I want to listen to the murmurings of my own spirit and then turn to the person next to me and ask, 'What does your spirit say to you?'

I tried over decades to fit these needs and longings into the religious language I inherited. 'Perhaps now I'll be *converted*,' I murmured hopefully, standing as a student at the door of the Christian Union meeting. 'Oh, for a *resurrection!*' I prayed, as yet again I lost faith – or was it that a sexual relationship had let me down? I begged God, 'May my friend be *saved*', and it was only later that I realised what my friend needed was not so much a dramatic salvation but the presence of human warmth and someone to listen to her in depth.

Eventually I began to ask myself, 'Why must you force your spirit into a mould? Why can't you let go, let the spirit blow where it wills and follow it where it leads?' Something Charles Morgan wrote speaks to me particularly: 'Miracles are not an arbitrary magic but a summoning of those reserves of nature which underlie common experience.'[3] My spiritual experience contains small miracles of that kind, and I'm searching for a language to express them.

Language as discovery

Where might I find this language? I can't say 'I have found it'. The finding is a process, not an achievement. What I can do is set out on an exploration, a voyage of discovery. And, though I don't know where I will end up, I do know where I can begin.

I begin with the language of human life. I want to find words which reflect everyday experience as nearly as possible in its original impact, rather than from the perspective of an existing theological interpretation. In a religious context, creeds and dogmas – together with the necessities of the institution itself – try to place an absolute meaning in the centre of life. This denies the subtle shifts of vision that happen in a split second, or over years of time. As a reader and a writer, as an individual and a friend, I have done my spiritual learning through my own and other people's direct experience, gained from deep sharing and from fiction and drama, biography and diaries and letters. These don't expect me to respond from a religious or moral standpoint. When I talk with another person at moments of crisis or at the point of realisation of some personal truth, there's no pre-set theological agenda, no assumption about how God meant the world to be. We take the world as it appears to us and try to make some kind of sense out of it. In this book I want to look at my life, and at the lives of ordinary and extraordinary people, real or fictional people, alive or dead, who have inspired me or infuriated me or even dogged my steps, and try to understand where the turning-points are, the spiritual discoveries, the moments of despair and exaltation, the abandonment and the hope. Because the journey is a process, my vision changes on the way.

'Everyday', 'human', 'common', 'ordinary': if I use words like these, does it mean that I have no sense of the eternal, that I'm searching for a language denuded of awe, of the transcendent, the mystical and sublime? I don't think so. It's just that I want to start from where I am, in life, in each day, in insight and relationship. Then I can move on when I'm ready, using the words of transcendence when it's clear that they are the ones I must use.

To take an example: at any moment, on any day, an accident might happen or an illness be diagnosed that faces me with the immediacy of death. This is by any definition an ultimate matter, an opportunity for the body to contemplate its spiritual nature without a moment's hesitation.

Here's an extract from my diary: 'Took Jennifer to Clatterbridge for radiotherapy. While we were there, something crystallised that's been forming in my mind since she was first ill: that if I had cancer I'd want to go to an "alternative" Cancer Help Centre and not to a conventional hospital. I said this to Frank and the girls over tea, and they reacted sharply. C asked if I was rejecting a "cure" in favour of a crank's solution. With F it went something like this:

> 'Me: I believe cancer is telling you something about your soul and your life-style.
> 'F: Yes, but that doesn't rule out science and surgery.

4

'Me: I don't want to have my hair fall out and little purple crosses marked all over me.

'F: But it sometimes works. People sometimes go on living because of it, instead of dying.

'Me: I believe that if you sort out your soul, your body will follow.

'F: Just because you believe something it isn't necessarily true.

'Later I felt cross at how inarticulate I'd been, faced with Frank's powers of argument. But I was moved that they were so upset at the thought of me rejecting treatment. It made me feel loved. I realised there are two Me's: one that, faced with death, imagines what her Meeting for Burial would be like: everyone flocking in, shocked and grieving and murmuring Wonderful-Alison-what-will-we-do-without-her. The other says: "I'm On My Own. Even though I accept my place in the world, and take responsibility for my little square of green, and want to leave it with a plus instead of a minus at the end of my saunter through . . . even so, there's no one going to do things for me but Me. I've got to make my own decisions and mop up after myself because there's no one else to do it for me". What I was trying to say to them, I think, was simply: I don't want the crisis of a life-threatening illness to make me ignore the needs of my soul in a frantic effort to save my body.

'Then suddenly the two Me's come together. I think, Here are three people – and more – who love me for myself and not for the functions or services I can perform. They love me, body *and* soul. So, though I am On My Own, I can't choose to die from my own misled autonomy (which I don't believe is misled, actually). I've got to take into account the feelings of the people who love me.'

Belief and experience

What I'm not going to attempt in this book is to find a liturgy, an alternative corporate language for a religious group to use when they meet together. This presents me with the problem of which pronoun to use. Liturgy uses 'We', and in early drafts of the book I used 'we' too. But that can be oppressive; it can assume consensus and agreement where actually there's difference and variety. So, in the main, I shall stick to 'I'. That involves the risk that I'll embark on an ego-trip. On the other hand, it means that the reader needn't take on board what I say, but can argue with it or offer an alternative at any time.

What I've found, as I've written and rewritten this book, is that the words we use in a spiritual context are a function of the relationship we have with each other, and the relationship we feel with the divine principle or the Spirit; and they are a function of our relationship to the movement of our own spirit within. It is these relationships I shall be exploring. I'm going to ask how it might be possible for me to express my spiritual being in terms of an inward process, in terms of what arises from within me and from my experience as I grow and change, instead of in terms of an outer purposeful agency to whom it is my duty to relate. I have a vision that, as the relationship with the spirit within becomes clear, then each individual is empowered to find their own words for the spiritual journey, together with the right medium for its expression. With that confidence, each can then find an increased sensitivity to the words of others, and to the spirit – whether a familiar or wholly different aspect of Spirit – that lies behind them.

One of the main things I want to question is the central concept of Western religious thought: the notion of *belief*. One of the mavericks of twentieth-century Quakerism, Ben Vincent, used to ask, 'What's the point of declaring that you believe something? If you believe it, then it will be obvious in your life. If it isn't obvious, then clearly your "belief" is hollow – mere words.'

This strikes me as wonderfully straightforward and sensible. What's the point in my saying, 'I believe in spiritual healing' if I rush to the pill-box every time I get a sneeze or a twinge? Where's the reality in my belief in life after death if I go into cold sweats every time I see a hearse?

'But', comes the response, 'if you don't believe anything, wherein lies your religion, your faith?'

Here is the challenge, to which the writing of this book is part of the answer. I am still feeling my way to a proper response. But this is the kernel of it:

I don't think that Belief need be the central concept of the spiritual life. Instead of believing, I want to respond in my life to all sorts of possibilities. I want to respond (to take the word 'faith' and flip it a little) to the possibility of *trust*. I can say to myself: Today I will respond to the world as if it were possible to trust it. I won't look at people with baleful eye, expecting them to trip me up and con me. I'll approach them like friends, like people who are valid, people who have secret hopes and talents. I'll look at the weather and the road conditions and the radio and TV schedules as if they've got something to offer, not something to offend me. I'll remember to ask the cat for a cuddle before I set out and trust her not to scratch. I'll even try to trust myself. Then I'll set off for the day. Some of my trust will be rewarded, some will be let down. But I feel confident that my openness to trust, and my own trustworthiness, will provoke a better response than if I believed in the world's inherent hostility, or even in God's ability to save me from all perils. Belief is a fixed position; trust is a way of being.

Take the extract from my diary about cancer. It's clear from a quick reading that I don't believe in the absolute power of doctors to cure cancer. I do believe that I have something called a 'soul' which is linked with my body but seems to have some existence outside it. It's also clear, when I look at the passage closely, that I've got to work quite hard at believing that people love me, but in the end I accept it as a fact. I don't seem to believe it's the responsibility of an outside agency to take care of my soul: that responsibility rests largely with me. But the care of my soul is affected by the love of other people.

These beliefs are not stated; there's no need to recite them. In the short term they emerged from my experience of going with a friend for treatment of a life-threatening illness and relating that to the prospect of my own death. In the longer term they must have emerged from my whole life's experience – body, mind, feelings and soul.

The search for an alternative to belief is linked to my life as a writer, and to my life as a reader of fiction and poetry and my experience as a theatre- and film-goer. If a writer 'believes in' what she writes, she begins to preach. If on the other hand she's open to possibilities, to imaginative leaps and journeys, then she can present people in the process of discovery, at a cusp in their lives, and enable the reader or audience to share the experience and be affected by it, even if it's in a different place from where they stand in their own lives. She can make her characters stand in all manner of places, with all manner of feelings far from, or even opposite to, her own and one another's: like George Eliot's Dorothea as she realises, at the very moment of loss of love for her dry and obsessive husband, that just as she has her own sense of self, he too has 'an equivalent sense of self, whence the lights and shadows must always fall with a certain difference'.[4]

Just as characters in a novel or a play can experience different experiences and believe different beliefs, yet each be faithful to themselves and be an indispensable part of a coherent whole, so my vision of spiritual reality is one that contains differences, even contradictions, within the tension of a whole that is larger than one person or group could ever hope for or conceive.

But the concept of fixed belief is so strong in our culture that even in the sphere of creativity you can trip up against it. When I wrote my radio play *Small Clouds Over Llangollen* I set half of it in heaven, half in North Wales, and interwove the two. Two characters, known simply as He and She, are souls waiting to reincarnate, and the husband-and-wife greengrocers in Llangollen are their eventual parents. So it was a 'what-if' play. But in order to enter fully into the 'what-if', I knew that I mustn't merely speculate; I mustn't try to be objective: 'If reincarnation really happened, then *this* would be the mechanism and *that* would follow.' If I only went that far I'd be standing outside the experiment and so would the audience. We'd all have a fascinating intellectual time and, if we'd listened to the play in company, we'd be discussing the pros and cons and ifs and buts for ages afterwards.

But no one would be moved; no one would feel that their personal vision had shifted a millimetre. So I had to go beyond the intellectual, beyond the question, to a more uncertain place: to an image-making of an answer.

The play was a comedy and everyone seemed to enjoy it. But people kept on asking me: 'Do you believe in reincarnation, then?'

I thought despairingly: Can religion never be experienced without this hard-edged tool of Belief? Can it not weave in and out of our lives gently, seamlessly, without party loyalties and categorisations? Emily Brontë didn't declare her belief in the power of a passionate gypsy to overturn the lives of generations of bourgeois women. E. M. Forster didn't sign a statement of faith in the healing properties of the Italian temperament and climate, or Sue Townsend give lifelong credence to the therapeutic power of diary-writing. These writers float themselves and their readers into an imaginative experience. They enter fully into it, as fully as if it were life itself. Then, after it's complete, writer and reader step back, breathe deeply, and ask: 'Now that I've perceived new experiences through different eyes and ears and feelings, what changes have taken place in the way my eyes see, my ears hear, my feelings respond?' Could our exchange of spiritual experiences not take the same course?

Where I come from

So what's the standpoint that I'm travelling from? That will become clear as the book progresses, but a faith-cum-denominational summary goes like this: I grew up in the Church of England, though my mother was a Congregationalist who changed to Anglicanism out of family solidarity. My parents sent me to a Methodist school, and when I was a student in Edinburgh it seemed sensible to go to the Presbyterian church with my friends there. At one point I almost converted to the Baha'i faith. Then in my mid-twenties I found my home among the Quakers and have stayed with them through the twenty or more years since. During that time I've shared experiences with a close friend, brought up a Quaker, who converted to Catholicism and considered becoming a postulant in a Religious Order; and with another who, in the search for her African roots, took a close and sympathetic look at Islam. Add a more recent friend who's a lifelong Muslim brought up in Lancashire, some Jewish friends, Yoga classes with an Indian teacher, and some delving into New Age thought and practice, and you witness the kind of hotchpotch that would inevitably make me wary of absolute answers, always ready to ask the opposite view.

In the Society of Friends and in my writing life, the act of listening to my own spirit and to the spirit of other people has become central. Quakers ask themselves to trust 'the promptings of love and truth in your heart . . . as the leadings of God'.[5] In researching a play or a book I may ask a complete stranger, 'Tell me about the most important moments in your life and what they mean for you.' Whenever this happens – if I'm listening properly, which isn't always – I hear something which convinces me that truth lies within each human being. Not Truth, but truth. This truth is never static. It's alive, dynamic, capable of absorbing contradictions, ready to move and challenge me in the deepest part of myself. It is whole, and not divided.

Something very deep inside me wants to be whole. It doesn't want to split into two: into higher and lower, carnal and spiritual, proper and improper. It feels a powerful urge to bring all of my life within a spiritual compass. Time and again I recognise this same urge in the novel I'm reading or the film or the play I'm watching – this passion for the spiritual in all things, in all feelings, in all events. Occasionally I recognise it in theology too: in feminist theologians, in the Creation Spirituality of Matthew Fox, and in personal stories like the one Canon Vanstone tells about his call to the ministry: 'An apple tree in the Vicarage garden bore a scant crop of which we were unreasonably proud. One day, seeing the branches of the tree shaken, I realised that the crop was being plundered; and I ran to protect it. The intruder also ran: but at the gate I caught him – a boy of about my own age. I grabbed at his arm to stop him: and I still remember the very thin wrist over which my hand closed. The boy wept; and said he was hungry; and pleaded with me to let him go. I let him go, saying nothing: but as I walked slowly back to the house the resolution formed in me that, if I could, I would follow my father's career.'[6]

I feel it most strongly when I turn to the person sitting beside me after the Quaker meeting for worship is over, and ask them how life is for them. They may say, 'I've come here for the first time because of inward promptings that I couldn't ignore any longer', or 'We've just found we're expecting another baby and I don't know how we'll cope'; or even 'Not so bad, thanks' – which might tell you that he can't concentrate on the meaning of life at the moment because his child is about to knock a grown-up's hot coffee all over herself.

Paradox and risk

When we start from the standpoint of where we are in our lives, and when we listen to other people or read about other lives in fiction, poetry, biography and drama, we're constantly knocked up, not against certainty, but against the tension of paradox. Whatever sense that emerges is unpredictable. Marion Milner found this in her delvings into the processes of her mind and heart: 'I began to have an idea of my life, not as the slow shaping of achievement to fit my pre-conceived purposes, but as the gradual discovery and growth of a purpose which I did not know. I wrote: "It will mean walking in a fog for a bit, but it's the only way which is not a presumption, forcing self into a theory." '7 There's the risk that no sense will emerge at all, that we'll feel ourselves drifting, sinking. That is part of the process.

The truth of what we see in this way is necessarily partial, because it's witnessed through individual eyes. It carries with it an ironic awareness: that even the simple act of looking at the world changes the world. An event twists and turns with every blink of the eye that sees it, every thought and feeling that interprets it. As each new insight is shoved on board, it alters the vision of why we are undertaking the voyage and what might be our ultimate destination. We might go to the door expecting to pay the milk bill, but someone is standing there with news that will change our lives.

As I've mentioned, I write a diary. I've kept it for years: I don't write it every day, just when the spirit moves. Sometimes the spirit doesn't move for weeks, then suddenly I write twenty pages at a sitting; in a few particular periods I've written the length of *War and Peace* in a few months. The process of writing shows me the flux that life thrusts on me. I try to shape it, to give it the satisfying cause-and-effect sequence that my intellect demands, but time and again that control, that sequence, elude me. Janet Frame says in her autobiography: 'The memories do not arrange themselves to be observed and written about, they whirl, propelled by a force beneath, with different memories rising to the surface at different times and thus denying the existence of a "pure" autobiography and confirming, for each moment, a separate story accumulating to a million stories, all different and with some memories staying forever beneath the surface. I sit here at my desk, peering into the depths of the dance, for the movement is dance with its own pattern, neither good nor bad, but individual in its own right.'8

The act of writing alerts me to the process of pattern-making.

It gives me the chance to look back, to perform a conscious offering of time and energy to the task of absorbing the events of the day or the week and my feelings towards them. It gives me the chance to catch a thought on the wing and follow it back to some sort of origin or connection. Sometimes the writing itself seems to be an act of sloughing off a skin or moving on to a new stage, so that I forget what I've written immediately it's on the page and when I reread it later I find it takes me by surprise. At times it gives me a warning: it shows me to what extent the need for shape and sequence determines my memory – even my perception – of the event. I take this to be warning of a larger danger: that once again the demand for Meaning is not only interpreting but actually creating my experience. Yet to speak of it as a 'danger' implies that I should be on my guard against it, should hold myself tightly under control to prevent this harmful process occurring . . . and at this point the tension breaks and I have to laugh at the contradictions I'm riding, like a posse of unruly horses over a stream.

Here's my diary trying to tackle that tension. 'Susan asked me, "If you're so much into meaninglessness, Alison, will you get rid of your diaries?" "Of course not!" I said, and she laughed. Nor, of course, will I stop all my other writing, which represents the struggle for meaning in the most focused way. I don't want to reject meaning, I just want to face squarely the fact that we, as human beings, search for meaning *because we need to* and not necessarily because there *is* any meaning. And not because Somebody dictates the meaning for us. Not that I reject mystery, the many mysteries: the beforeness and afterness I sense in life, the non-physical communications; the intricacy of the natural world, which is a mystery utterly. I reject – have no experience of, and much experience/knowledge of its non-being – the notion that the force behind all creation is working actively to bring good out of us. At the moment I think chance operates a lot. I think it's a hotch-potch of purpose and chance.'

The exercise of journal- or diary-keeping is a key to the purpose of this book. It's an act in itself, but it's also a metaphor. My hope is that, in writing the diary and in writing this book, I can develop an attitude of *spiritual reflectiveness*. Each experience can be reflected on as an opportunity for spiritual growth: any event, any emotion, any relationship – its faults and fears as well as its creativity – can be absorbed into the whole as a new impulse for movement and an ingredient for change. There may be no immediate insight that arises, no direct moral connection like, 'I was wrong, I was hurtful; I resolve to do better next time'. The process may evolve in the unconscious mind, or in the movement of the spirit at a deeper level. Sometimes, as with the journal-writing, the reflection will melt away and be absorbed and forgotten. Often we won't be able to comment or interpret at all, but can accept the experience as sufficient in itself.

Many years ago I spent a day with a friend, Elisabeth. She and I were both bereaved, and by the same cause: a close friend and colleague had died very suddenly. There seemed at the time to be no sense in this death: just a gaping hole where that friend should have been. We were both thrown up against grinding, interminable questions. Had we done all that we could? Should we have done differently? How could we cope with the new situation? How was it even possible, looking back, to make sense of the life that had preceded it? Neither of us could find in our religious background any sure footing to help us.

At some point in the day Elisabeth said, 'You remember that book I told you you simply must read?' I didn't remember anything about it, but such was the confusion of the day that I answered, 'Yes, of course. What about it?' She said, 'I've found a copy.' She put into my hand a book she'd picked out of one of the cardboard boxes you see outside second-hand shops that contain the books that are too cheap and tatty to keep on the shelves inside. It was *A Fortunate Man* by John Berger, with photographs by Jean Mohr.[9] In words and in pictures it tells the story of a family doctor who works alone in a large, economically depressed country area. He is a good doctor, professional and open. He is a reflective man, observing himself and his patients while he works, and he knows that in healing others he also heals himself. I'll include an extract from the book in a later chapter to show the quality of his life.

I don't know what it was about the story of this individual life that gave me such insight and help at a critical time. Maybe it was because it stretched my imagination in an unexpected direction. Maybe it was because the depth and emotional danger of this man's life found echoes in my own. It was only years afterwards that I realised how profound was its effect on me, and that it made me see that I'd always searched books, poems, plays

13

and films for the sort of paradoxical truth, the truth-with-many-faces that I found in the depth of my own life, and that friends and strangers had communicated to me in a million different ways.

The writing of this book is an extension of that search. It gives me the chance to share the search, and it urges me to carry on the exploration into new and as yet unmapped territory. The process of writing has deepened and broadened the task, because I've been encouraged to follow the path marked out by other 'wounded pilgrims' and share at some depth the experiences that have shaped my personal journey. The aim of this book, as of the others in the series, is to bring both the writer and the reader to a place they might not have recognised at the beginning.

I hope that this journey of personal, spiritual, linguistic exploration can be a springboard and support for the reader's own journey of discovery. First I will explore a language for the individual spiritual journey, reclaiming what has been traditionally the sphere of the scriptures and the prayer book in search of words and forms that can express what each human being can find on their own. Then I'll start to focus on what we as individuals can say to each other, how we can listen to each other, how we can sense when our spirit is leading us beyond words; and, as the book draws towards its end, ask how it might be possible to create a spiritual community in which differences can be celebrated rather than feared, and the whole be known as greater than the sum of its parts.

> 'And we could put blank pages between the chapters – between pages – between paragraphs, even . . .'
> '*Blank*?'
> 'So that readers could write "Oh! It was different for me." And then *how* it was different. They could write their own book . . .'
> 'Yes.' (Patiently.) 'That's the theme, I can see that. But I'm afraid the economics of publishing make it out of the question.'
> 'Maybe we could sell it with a free note-book attached . . .'
> (*Fictional exchange between AL and DLT*)

14

2

LET ME BE WARMED

Your pier-glass or extensive surface of polished steel made to be rubbed by a housemaid, will be minutely and multitudinously scratched in all directions; but place now against it a lighted candle as a centre of illumination, and lo! the scratches will seem to arrange themselves in a fine series of concentric circles round that little sun. It is demonstrable that the scratches are going everywhere impartially, and it is only your candle which produces the flattering illusion of a concentric arrangement, its light falling with an exclusive optical selection. These things are a parable. The scratches are events . . .

(GEORGE ELIOT, *Middlemarch*)

God has always been a character inside my head. Sometimes he's been principal protagonist; often he's been antagonist; sometimes abstract as a Mondrian painting, full of bright meaningless colours and parallel straight lines going nowhere. Often he's been a character off-stage, identifiable only by my knowledge that his presence – or absence – influences the action. Even now, when I can't declare in an orthodox Christian sense that I 'believe in God', I still catch myself sensing God as a kind of Sin Monitor, a cosmic school prefect who's spotted me running across the spiritual grass or laughing when I should be demure.

The God who entered in at the earliest, unremembered moments of my self-awareness is a character as complex as any in Pinter or Chekhov. He has features given to him by the adults in my life out of their need for order and discipline, plus features I've given him myself from my projection and fantasy, plus features of his own that I must have absorbed through the pores as I went to church and chapel and heard people talking about

15

this entity called God. He was always a 'he': not necessarily adorned with beard and hairy chest and god-knew-what under his robes, but powerfully masculine in the sense that he didn't have to ask what to be, he just *was*. '*I am that I am*': what woman, what girl, would be able to say that? How could I, little me, say simply, 'I am'?

Original impotence

In a contrary sort of way, this God of power who made me feel helpless and small could also, at times, give me power. Though I was only 'little me' or 'silly Ali' – phrases that recur, originating in my being the youngest of three and a sucker for teasing – even I could be imbued with the characteristics of the Almighty. It was a wonderful kind of paranoia: delusions of persecution joined with delusions of fantastic grandeur, the need that every child has to say, despite all evidence to the contrary, 'I am the boss'.

My first conscious memory of this God character is one of these contrary combinations of helplessness and power. When I was eight years old, we were staying in a caravan on Achill Island off the coast of County Mayo in the Republic of Ireland. The sand there is almost white and can be cut into shapes like cake. My family were comfortably off and were among the earliest and most adventurous caravanners. The caravan wasn't rented, it was our own, and Mother had taken photos of it being winched up in a great sling and nudged across, high above the void, from the quay on to the ferry at Liverpool Docks. So we were alone on Achill Island, just Mother and Daddy and my older brother and sister and me. On this occasion I must have done something Mother disapproved of, I can't remember what, and many years later I expressed my feelings in the form of a poem:

> 'I am God,' I said. Gritty and damp,
> the sand met my knees. 'Yes I am God.'
> Pouting, being eight years old,
> disgraced from the caravan,
> I turned my bucket upside down,
> viewed my creation and saw
> that it was good.
> 'I shall kneel here on the sand

until the tide comes and washes me away.
And I shall send my angel
who will flap its vasty wings at them
and tell them the eternal truth –
that I am God. Then they will wail,
and grovel, and kneel down on the damp
and gritty sand, and worship me.'
Then
I took the kitchen spoon in my powerful square hand,
and dug, and filled my bucket once again.[1]

Our lives begin in helplessness: not so much 'original sin' as 'original impotence'. Our memories and feelings are forged in that early crucible. We are nourished and punished; we have the world described and explained to us; the world is offered as *given*. There is no alternative. Power structures are built into our relationships from the very beginning. Subtle, all-pervasive, they are kept in place by internal and external fears. Adults, preoccupied with their own needs and crises, can't see the crying need of children.

Writing for children, I see children's literature as full of the impotence and fantastic power of small people. In the children's classics the lives of heroes and heroines are either totally independent, played out in an adult-free world which they can themselves control, or their destiny is determined by larger Beings who give no reasons and expect complete and immediate compliance. Lewis Carroll's Alice is either a giant, or tiny and at life's mercy: 'She soon made out that she was [swimming] in the pool of tears which she had wept when she was nine feet high.'[2] Christopher Robin, friend of Winnie-the-Pooh and Piglet and Eeyore, seems the essence of power and wisdom to his small stuffed friends, but finally he is wrenched from them and sent off by an unspecified authority to an unknown destination far away.[3]

As children we exercise no power except by means of loud and often useless protest. But we know that protest might lead to rejection – life and folk-tale are full of fearsome examples – and ever wilder protest can lead to greater anxiety and repression from the wretched parents, or even a visit to the child psychiatrist. Most of us learn to please, and become the Good Child. Often, when parents refer to a baby as 'good', they mean one who sleeps most of the time. How I used to admire the rare tough child who could somehow develop and maintain an independent stand.

These beings called Grown-Ups who loom over our lives and lovingly wreak on us their well-meant decisions easily become confused with God. Edmund Gosse's father was a strict Evangelical, and the young Edmund experienced this confusion in a highly concentrated form. 'My Mother always deferred to my Father, and in his absence spoke of him to me, as if he were all-wise. I confused him in some sense with God; at all events I believed that my Father knew everything and saw everything. One morning in my sixth year, my Mother and I were alone in the morning-room, when my Father came in and announced some fact to us. I was standing on the rug, gazing at him, and when he made this statement, I remember turning quickly, in embarrassment, and looking into the fire. The shock to me was as that of a thunderbolt, for what my Father had said "was not true" . . . Here was the appalling discovery, never suspected before, that my Father was not God, and did not know everything.'[4]

Long into adulthood, key concepts of religion like sin, judgement and punishment can revive childish feelings of helplessness in the face of All-mighty Power. For me, when I was an Anglican, the words 'I have sinned, through my own fault, through my own most grievous fault . . . And there is no health in me' were indistinguishable from 'You're a naughty, naughty child and you can't come downstairs again till you're good'.

But God wasn't always the Cosmic Tyrant. He could be the Mighty Comforter, the one who saw and understood the anguish or talent that everyone else had failed to notice, a shelter against the storm, a haven of mercy when the world of adults rejected me. As a child I used to pour out my troubles to this unseen Power each night, inside my head, as we sat on imaginary rocking chairs on either side of a great log fire. The beauty of God was that he could be all things to everyone, and all sorts of different things to me. While there was plenty of the punitive about God, especially as I went into adolescence, most of my early feelings were of him being *on my side*.

One of my adult daughters, who has no religious belief in the straightforward sense, asked me recently in a tone of genuine puzzlement what brought about my devotion to Jesus when I was a child. I went to the piano and sang the hymn that used to inspire in me such trust:

> It is a thing most wonderful,
> almost too wonderful to be,
> that God's own Son should come from heaven
> and die to save a child like me.[5]

Imagine: God's own Son, for me! Though I had to add that there was sometimes a lurking fear to undermine the trust. What if the Mighty Comforter should be displeased, withdraw his favours and throw me into the pit? I can still have flashbacks to that terror and helplessness, when I seem to be standing on the edge of madness. Occasionally, in hushed concerts or crowded stations, or in gatherings of the Great and the Good, or even in a Quaker Meeting, I am pierced with fear that I'll be propelled to my feet and scream and swear and have to be dragged out of the room and off to the 'bin', or that I might rush forward and fall in front of an approaching train. I can trace this feeling back to childhood incidents when I sensed that my parents, who should be like God and therefore always present and strong to care for me, were in fact chaotic themselves: out of control, furious, wild, mad. Of course their chaos was hidden from me; they thought I hadn't noticed it. Because they perceived me as a small and ignorant child – and probably because they thought I was asleep, or pre-occupied with play – they assumed I wouldn't see their panic and their fear. But I did, as children always do. I sensed that the All-Powerful was in fact impotent like myself.

Maybe this is one source of the rush to authoritarianism that happens when someone, or some group – whether feminists, or green or peace protesters, or people who are HIV-positive – are perceived as a threat to the established order. It evokes a childhood terror of unspoken chaos, and so provokes the demand that order, any order, be reimposed immediately. In the church this panic reveals itself in the rejection of radical thinkers like David Jenkins, in the attempts to ban films like *The Life of Brian* and *The Last Temptation of Christ*, in *fatwas* of any kind.

Eternity and rules

I went to boarding school at the age of eight, and everything changed. I knew I had to be good, and not be myself; in fact, I wondered who 'myself' could be, and tried out lots of different ideas of my identity, both inside myself and outside in the world. God, the God of the rocking chair, could be with me inside my head, listening to me quietly beside the great log fire, nodding, and I think (though this may be a later accretion) stroking His long grey beard, understanding everything. Later this God transformed Himself into fantasy versions of actual people who also understood everything. Later still these people evolved from fantasies of total comprehension into more real versions of their living selves, and these more real individuals would argue with me, tell me I'd got it wrong, and put their point of view in such a forceful manner that I couldn't run away with the idea that my view was sole and paramount. Talking with other writers who have grown up in institutions, several have told me that their fantasy life in these places must have been the origin of their life as a writer.

But that was much later. My first God-person was a receptacle only, a piece of heavenly blotting paper to soak up all my confusions and mirror them back to me as *all right*.

I suppose that in psychological terms this rocking-chair God communicated itself to me as a sense of self-worth. It seems a kind of grace that this aspect should have been present to balance the more punitive side. It told me that my spirit existed: that it had space to exist, if only inside my head, in the dark, when no one else was looking; and that its space couldn't be invaded or destroyed.

Outside that conviction, everything was confused. At school there was no home territory, no street gang of which I, though the tiniest, could be a part; no safe sounds of traffic at night, or small bedroom with just my sister and me. Here were vast dining halls where the most essential regulation was announced just at the moment I'd stopped listening. Here were dormitories and rules and unhappy housemistresses. The housemistress of my first term put her head in a gas oven during the Christmas holidays.

I've no specific recollection, when I remember these scenes, that I felt abandoned by my parents to the institution. But in later years I've learnt that my awareness of being abandoned as a child has been a key factor in my feelings about myself and about other people. It fills me with longing for the unity which was broken at that time. My spiritual search has been in some measure a search for that unity, and I recognise it clearly and painfully in other people.

Each morning in Assembly and, in longer doses, on Sunday morning and evening, God took his place in our school lives. He was mediated by men, the only men we ever saw. Men dressed in dark suits with white dog-collars visited the school chapel regularly to interpret the eternal, via the stories of the Bible and their own anecdotes, in the hope of making it relevant to our sheltered little lives. The overwhelming memory of those years is of boredom. Into this boredom descended the clergy, and I loved them because I knew they brought real things. They told us about Africa, hot and wet and jungly, where our contributions in the collection box would go, and about Palestine, hot and dusty, where Jesus walked. One Scripture teacher managed to point out, despite her embarrassment, that Mary had given birth to the baby Jesus without benefit of midwife or clean towels. I remember one itinerant preacher telling us about a winter train journey he'd taken in the course of duty to the north of Scotland, and how the train's heating system failed, and he'd watched a drop of condensation freeze on the inside of the window next to him, and how exquisite it was, making him marvel at the beauty of God's creation.

The ethos among the girls demanded that we mock or ignore these contributions, but privately I revelled in them. I was no good at being a child, at relaxing and having fun and not minding being teased. I knew deep down that I'd be better off when I became a grown-up and could be, without it being bayed as an insult, 'serious'. I knew these clergyman were trying to talk about Real Life, real questions of Morality and Meaning and Eternity. But, at the same time, what they were saying from the pulpit to us in our hard pews ('twelve to a row, eleven if it's Sonia Drayton') could be summed up as: 'Listen to us. We know. We are men, and we dress in this special way. What we do during the week is a mystery, but on a Sunday we come here to tell you what life is all about and how to behave. You're not allowed to argue. You can't ever get up in the pulpit yourselves to tell *us* what *you* think life is all about. Just listen. Be passive. Be good. God is all around.

He watches you. We are His representatives. God owns the world, but since you can't see Him, think of us as being God.'

Here must be the origin of the Sin Monitor, the cosmic police-man with x-ray eyes and an endless capacity to punish and con-demn. The 'children's sermons' from these Methodist preachers were benign, but the language of the Bible, the hymns, the adult homily, and the morning assemblies where the acceptable and unacceptable were delineated in particular and public form, made plain the message: that our especial contribution to the spiritual life was unquestioning obedience.

The confusion that these mixed messages aroused in me is the source of a rage that can still grip me as I walk along the street and see a perfectly harmless clergyman walking towards me on some business of his own. 'What right have *you* to tell me how to run my life!' I want to shriek at him – 'Parasite! Hypocrite!' when the poor man is probably just popping along to the dentist with a painful abscess or out in his lunch hour from a gruelling day on 'How the Church must face up to AIDS'. There's a sense of betrayal in my rage. As a child I asked them for glimpses of eternity, and what I got from them was rules.

Sheila Rowbotham, who was in the year ahead of me at the same school, recounts a different memory.[6] The east coast of Yorkshire gets biting winds and chilling 'sea frets', and in the winter the school buildings were fearfully cold. Sheila was more practical than me. She knelt down on the wooden floor in the east Yorkshire winter, praying: 'God, if you exist, let me be warmed.' God didn't, so she concluded that He didn't exist. That was it for God.

It's curious that within the same couple of years this school and its chapel should have produced Sheila Rowbotham, the Marxist feminist thinker, myself as a writer and Quaker, and Vivienne Welburn, playwright and author of an excellent book on post-natal depression. Clearly the environment either encouraged us to articulate, or failed to prevent us articulating, or even by sheer frustration forced us to articulate, the different truth as each of us saw and felt it.

During the holidays my sister and I were taken on Sunday to the parish church where my father was a faithful sidesman. He had always been an Anglican, while my mother was raised a Congregationalist; but at some point in my childhood Mother took instruction and joined the Anglicans too, though she seldom went to services because the pews were too hard for her slight, unhealthy frame. I remember being amazed that my all-knowing mother could be instructed about anything. She sent my sister and me to the Methodist boarding school because of its reputation among some of their friends, but in adolescence we too took instruction in the Anglican faith, coming home for special days to go for an hour to the dank unwelcoming home of a deaconess who reminded me uncomfortably of the suicidal housemistress of my first term. The parish church was light and airy, overwhelmingly sky blue, and we followed our father's movements as he stood and sang, knelt and prayed. I described an adolescent's response to this church in *An Inch of Candle*: 'As she faced the altar, with its embroidered cloth and orange gold crosses, she thought momentarily of God. The God who lived here received rich, formal, repetitive prayer. The God who lived at chapel got more variety – but did He miss the eloquence, the unity of voice, the weight of centuries of authority? The God who listened in these rafters must be a very orderly and ancient one. He would know exactly what was what. He wouldn't thrash about endlessly over moral problems like Mr Lofthouse's God at the chapel seemed to do. This God would be stalwart against cowardice, upright as a pillar in the midst of pettiness and vice.'[7]

I don't remember anything of the sermons. The prayers and the creed I can recite to this day: 'We have done those things which we ought not to have done, we have left undone those things which we ought to have done . . .' and 'I BELIEVE IN GOD, THE FATHER ALMIGHTY, MAKER OF HEAVEN AND EARTH, AND IN JESUS CHRIST HIS ONLY SON OUR LORD . . .' The creed was always in capital letters. We looked up at the glorious stained glass as we recited it. I didn't know anyone in that church; we went to Sunday School there for a while, but often had weekends away in the Lake District, where my parents were keen mountaineers. On one occasion my sister and I concocted a lie about how many times we'd attended Sunday School so that we could go on the Summer Outing. Being at boarding school during term-time loosened times at home. Home was a place you went to visit, for holidays. When you came back you wrote a letter of thanks to your parents for having given you such a nice time, which was vetted by the presiding teacher.

The language of the prayer book and the creed entered into my veins at a very early age. I can't remember when I wasn't aware that I'd 'erred and strayed from Thy ways like a lost sheep' through 'my own fault – my own grievous fault', or when phrases like 'devices and desires' and 'without form and void' didn't echo around my brain – though I somehow missed the fact that 'void' was an adjective; I always thought it was another thing that the earth was without. When I was a little-girl-lost at school, sayings like 'God so loved the world that He gave His only begotten Son' were a blanket of comfort to me.

I was a musical child, too. So the beauty of Stainer's melodies carried the 'only begotten Son' up into the heavenly sphere, and on a more mundane level I knew, because I sang it so vigorously, that I had a 'Friend in Jesus' 'above the bright blue sky'. I had promised to 'serve Him to the end' because I had 'surveyed the wondrous Cross' and 'Truly', as Johann Sebastian Bach told me, 'this was the Son of God'.

As I write them in a string like that I can feel a wave of hindsighted cynicism sweeping over me. I'm tempted to accuse the church of seducing me into religious belief by taking up my fragile emotions and channelling them through words and music into religiosity instead of into more 'normal' childhood preoccupations like friendship and play. But I can't accuse anyone of leading me astray. This was the kind of child I was, and that was the setting into which I was thrown, and the combination just turned out like that.

The power of the absent

It was while I was taking instruction for confirmation that my religiosity burst through in minor rebellion. As an Anglican preparing for confirmation I was allowed to go home for periods of instruction; but as a pupil at a Methodist boarding school I was supposed to obey the rules. As a passionately religious adolescent I felt I was above the rules and I sneaked out one afternoon, when I ought to have been playing netball or lacrosse, to go through the back gate of the school and pray in the Anglican church across the village street from the school grounds. How trivial it seems now, to set one denomination against another. But it didn't seem adolescent and trivial; it didn't seem like the Key

To All the Mysteries either; it was just something I had to do. The history teacher was my current heroine, and I wanted the God of History – the God for whom the pews were carved by a man who wrote no poetry except what he carved into the foot pedestals and the prayer-book stands, the God for whom the organ sounded, 'We praise Thee, oh God, we acknowledge Thee to be the Lord' – not the God of the school who put me in a felt hat with a stringy thread of elastic under the chin to hold it on my head against the biting East Yorkshire wind.

I'd only got just outside the gate, I hadn't even got across the road, when who should be walking towards me but the much-disliked headmistress. A sportswoman gone to seed, murmured her sympathisers, who were few. 'Well – er – ' – she never remembered names – 'what do you think you're doing here?'

I can't remember how I was punished. The real punishment came when the history teacher wrote on my end-of-term report: 'Alison must learn that rules are for the benefit of the community and must be obeyed.' Not only had my heroine humiliated me; I then had to explain to my angry mother what her words meant. I couldn't explain except in terms of a brainstorm. Upstairs on my bed, raging and beating the pillow, I knew there was a reason. I can't even now articulate what it was, except in terms of a need for poetry and for mystery. How could I say this to adults, who never understood? In fact it was the history teacher herself who seemed the nearest to understanding, because from then on she treated me as an adult, debating with me all sorts of knotty questions such as whether it would have been morally right to kill Hitler if you had the chance. She argued with an intensity that broke for a few moments the hierarchy of all-wise teacher and ever-humble child.

When, not long afterwards, I came to be confirmed, I entered into it with all the passion of a confused and idealistic teenager. I can write those words coolly, but the feelings come rushing back to deny the coolness. I *am* that teenager, I'm still seething with those confusions and idealisms. I went home for my confirmation – a fact of much curiosity to my Methodist friends, as my visits for instruction had been, too. I dressed myself up with a suitable blend of specialness and modesty and walked with head bowed in the middle of a procession of unknown companions into the parish church. The Bishop of Selby, a gentle man of great humanity, confirmed us in our membership of Christ's Church. He spoke sincerely about our lives: this being the turning-point, the moment when we gave ourselves to God; and he laid his hands on each head. I remember the touch. I was proud and humbled. I felt certain that I was giving myself, body and soul, to the divine imperative.

But when I got back to school I was hurled into disillusion. The girls absorbed me back without comment. They'd forgotten the specialness of my absence and regaled me with all sorts of trivialities, gossip and demands. Didn't they realise, I wondered, that I was different now? The bitter truth hit me like a brick hitting glass. I *wasn't* different now. Or rather, I was still different-peculiar rather than different-special. I took a look inside my head and saw, drawn there graphically, the fantasy that had been sustaining me: that my confirmation as an Anglican, different from these dull Methodists, with all the Anglican light and colour and sonorous words and laying on of hands in a direct line from St Peter, would confer on me a magic that would enable me to be sweet and saintly without having to make any effort at all. More, I would suddenly be popular without having to be good at sport and even while wearing the spectacles that I'd had to use for the last couple of years because of short sight.

It evaporated, the fantasy. I was just the same brainy, mouldy, teased-for-being-serious Alison that I'd always been. The magic hadn't worked, it hadn't 'taken'. So much for induction, ceremony, ritual. I'd asked the external God to come into my life and, for the first but certainly not for the last time, it seemed that He'd decided to remain absent.

The boarding school was based on an old manor house, and its ethos was that of the manor system. Hereditary dynasties provided the names for what other public schools called 'houses'; we had 'stewards' instead of prefects, 'seneschals' to administer discipline, and pseudo-medieval 'Courts Leet' where those to be disciplined were reprimanded in public. There was a modern quadrangle where the main body of the school lived and studied, but the little ones were housed in the old manor house itself, a dark-corridored, oak-panelled house covered all over with Virginia creeper. The headmistress had her study here and the staff their private hideaway, and upstairs the 8-to-10-year-olds slept on iron bedsteads, eight to a room. It was by no means Do-The-Girls Hall. My parents had chosen it over other schools because teddy-bears were allowed in bed, and the headmistress seemed affectionate and knowledgeable about the girls. But I wasn't interested in teddy-bears and the head retired a couple of years after I got there, giving way to the ex-sportswoman who had no interest in pupils other than her favourites.

The school had been founded for the education of daughters of Methodist missionaries, which seemed in its time – and even in my time, when missionaries' daughters weren't enough to fill the school to viability – a noble aim. But my first term wasn't out before I learnt the down-side of Mission: that if you decide to – in religious language 'are called to' – serve God and one particular distant section of humanity, then you must make difficult choices. And the choice may be that you can't properly serve another, closer, section of humanity: your family.

In my first term I slept in a bed next to a girl six months older than me, called Hilary, who was just nine and wore her crinkly fair hair long because her father didn't like his wife and four daughters to cut their hair. She was an exceptionally sweet yet self-contained child, a girl whom it didn't occur to us to tease. Even her long plaits didn't get pulled, though when it came to hair-washing nights we begged her to go to the end of the queue because her thick-textured mass took so long for the poor housemistress to shampoo and rinse. And to dry, too. I remember one happy term – perhaps the term after the suicide – when a temporary housemistress was inspired to light a fire in a small common room and we knelt beside it to dry our dripping hair while she read us stories. We tried to get nearer the fire than Hilary because her hair took up so much room, and we laughed at the housemistress behind her back, I remember, because she pronounced 'bush' to rhyme with 'rush'. I felt ashamed of joining in the laughter, but joined in all the same. I can't remember which stories she told or read to us, but since then I've always loved listening to stories, and reading them aloud to my children or anyone else who will listen.

One night, in the darkness of the panelled room, I heard Hilary crying. This was strange because Hilary hadn't seemed to be homesick. (How we laughed at Angie, who wept with homesickness all the time.) I got out of bed and went to her. Trying – and miraculously succeeding – both to cry and to talk without waking

27

anyone else up, she told me that this was the night when her father and her mother were sailing for India with her three younger sisters, and they wouldn't come back for five years. There they would live and work in 'the compound' and help 'the natives' to understand about Jesus and God. It was important work, she understood that; but she was miserable about it because she would miss them. I asked, where would she go in the holidays? To various aunts, she said; and I conjured up images of tall gaunt women with wiry hair scraped back into tight buns. Five years! Five Christmases – five summers – three half-terms and three holidays a year . . . six-fives-are-thirty visits to the wire-haired aunts, and not a cuddle or a smile! So said my imagination. I knelt down beside Hilary and did what my mother did to me when I was ill: I murmured soothing words and stroked her hair.

I didn't of course know anything about the politics of religion at the time, but the impact of that night's exchange was never to leave me. Looking back with the benefit of training in psychology and some personal psychotherapeutic counselling, I understand now that I identified with Hilary in her sense of abandonment by her parents because I was abandoned by mine too. But I could see that hers was a very special sort of abandonment, because God had demanded that she should be abandoned in favour of a more deserving cause. *His* cause. God needed Hilary's misery so that the natives outside the compound could be happy, could be saved.

And I knew that this was wrong. I knew that *God* was wrong: that if He'd intended the natives to have Hilary's mummy and daddy for His own, then He should have been sensible enough to make Hilary's mummy and daddy decide not to produce children at all, and that if they did have children, then those children needed loving just as much as the natives – in fact they needed more, because there were other people to love the natives whereas there was no one else to love Hilary. I knew that Hilary deserved love – I suppose, that I deserved love too – and that God was depriving her of it, deliberately, almost purposefully. Hilary was sweet and meek and she accepted that this was the way life was. But I didn't. I took her misery on board and made it my own, and I hated her God for inducing it.

I recently had an idea for a play. The setting would be this East Yorkshire boarding school, and the theme of the play would be *the power of the absent*. There would be three layers to the piece.

The first layer would be historical, and would show the events that we girls portrayed every few years in an outdoor pageant called *The Saga*. The opening scene was the one in which the natives of Yorkshire demonstrated their allegiance to their absent Danish conquerors by ceremonially flinging a javelin out from the cliff top over the sea. The second scene would show the women and girls of this semi-convent demonstrating, by lust and obeisance, their loyalty to the absent Male. The third layer would be religious. Mortal beings would wrestle with the necessity of bending their feeble wills to the greater will of the most absolute absence of all, the absence of God.

INTERVAL

❧ *A Day in the Life of an Unbeliever* ❧

March 1994. 7 a.m. I wake, warm and comfortable, in a
Christian conference centre in windswept North Wales.
There's been snow followed by a rapid thaw, and the gracious
parkland is churned up by cattle hooves. A few snowdrops
dangle in a copse above the lake, early daffodils are budding
in the garden. The management is deeply Christian and the
staff serve us lovingly without pressing their views on us. On
the walls hang exquisite landscape photographs decorated
with prayers and biblical quotations. The one in our bedroom
is a pounding surf saying, 'Lord, fill me with your love'. I
argue inside my head. Why not 'Lord, fill me with *love*'?
The argument goes on: why not '*Fill* me with love'? Then,
'*Let me be filled* with love'. Then, '*May I be filled* with love'.
Then, 'I flipping well hope to be filled with love'.

Breakfast. There are ninety of us here, a third of them
children. There's a certain quality of parenting that I notice:
a willingness to listen to each child, an absence of 'Because
I say so'. I know some of these parents well; I know that
they can get frantic and angry with their children. But they
have an aim, a base line of loving communication held on
to through a busy routine so that it can blossom in a relaxed
and nurturing setting like this one. I look over at Pete, a
nine-year-old tearaway. He's had a phase of clambering into
his mother's bed in the early hours of the morning to whis-
per, 'If we're born and then we die, what's the point?'

After teeth-brushing, nappy-changing, and sorting bed-
rooms and chairs for the oldies who have arthritis and bad
backs, we meet for worship in the Round Room. There's
bustle, gossip, children playing with electronic-noise-making
toys, people coming in and, realising they've forgotten a

hankie, out and back in again. Then someone signals to close the door.

Worship. As Quakers we talk about 'meeting for worship'. Who or what do we worship? Quite a lot of the older generation can talk easily about God, and a few of the younger. Many practise individual meditation to find their inward stillness. George Fox talked about the Inner Light, the Seed. We don't analyse the word 'worship'; we ignore the word's transitive nature, the fact that you can't strictly speaking set about *worship* without worshipping *something*. Yet, as the meeting begins, we fall silent and, most of the time, we know what we're doing. We're finding the centre of ourselves, the heart of things, the truth of life, the love, that can't be expressed in words.

After ten minutes or so someone speaks: a couple of sentences about the value of having the children in meeting for worship.

Quiet. Outside the rooks are cawing and the wind sweeps across the hills. 'The wind bloweth where it listeth.' I think of the childhood sermon which told me that in its original language 'wind' could also be translated as 'spirit': *the spirit moves where it feels inclined.*

Someone speaks about Elijah: the Lord was not in the wind, nor in the earthquake, nor in the fire; but after the fire there came a still, small voice. I think of singing Mendelssohn's *Elijah* with our Unitarian friends in Philadelphia; then of their friend Zeke, serving life for murder; of his search for God through Islam, and for his 'real self' who can forgive and be forgiven.

The younger children have become restless and someone has taken them out. Someone else speaks; it washes over me. I'm in a state of transition, of waiting. I'm empty, and it feels risky. My heart beats very loud, then quietens, then thumps again. I feel irritated that I have to put up with this alternation. What's happening? I don't know. I just have to wait.

After a while it's time to shake hands.

Pause.

Gillian now tells us about the creative things we're going to do in the next day and a half. A year ago she offered to develop a play on the theme of 'Pilgrimage', taking John

31

Bunyan as her model because *Pilgrim's Progress* was a favourite book. Then she reread it and found it full of sermonisings and denunciations of Popery. 'Hang on,' I think, 'some of us here have best friends who are Catholic, and they would never describe their faith as *Popery*.' Then I admit that Bunyan was a man of his time; anti-Catholicism was the name of the religious game in the seventeenth century, and in the twentieth we have left most of that, though not all, behind.

So, Gillian has written for us a-skip-and-a-hop through *Pilgrim's Progress*. She divides us into four groups: actors, musicians, scenery-makers, and those who chicken out of the dramatic process and go to a quiet room to discuss the philosophy and spirituality of pilgrimage. I choose scenery-making. The teenagers set about making the Celestial City, little Jim and his step-father get to work on the mythical Apollyon, and I'm in charge of turning a crowd of small boys into hobgoblins and foul fiends. We cut up boxes to make masks, beg some black binliners from the kitchen, paint cardboard tails black and tie them on with string. Before long Josh has invented a devil's mask with an articulated lower jaw that actually goes up and down as he speaks.

In the spaces while we're waiting to borrow the scissors or for paint to dry, some of the adults wonder what a police report might say if they decided to swoop today. We're aware of the Orkney case of alleged satanic child abuse in which a Quaker family were involved. When they described their meetings for worship – 'We sit quietly in a circle, waiting for the voice of God' – the police interpreted it as witchery, devil-worship. And what were the early Christians accused of as they developed the sacrament of Holy Communion? Cannibalism. 'The body and blood of Christ, which was given for you . . .' I suspect that George Fox, were he to wander about now as he did in the seventeenth century marching into 'steeple-houses' and interrupting sermons with an accusing shout, would be locked up and pumped with Largactyl. 'He *was* locked up,' Jack points out. 'In prison, not psychiatric hospital.' Well, there are dungeons and dungeons. David Icke said that if Christ were to return today there'd be no need to crucify him. He'd just be ridiculed in the tabloids and that would do the trick.

2 p.m. After lunch, gangs go off swimming or up a mountain. I opt for a bit of peace by myself. Several others are doing the same. Are they feeling left out of the cosy cliques, or wanting peace like I am? I can't cope with the question and walk round the grounds with my camera. I'm a novice photographer. I notice with amusement how photographers get gripped by an almost religious fervour, discussing concepts of exposure compensation, depth of field and backlighting in reverent voices. I'm a novice theologian too. I grasp both sets of concepts fully and easily at times, then suddenly find them evaporating into thin air.

Back to the house, where two strangers, astray from their walk, have wandered in and been offered tea. We try to explain who we are. 'A sort of church . . . not a church . . .' Christian? 'Er . . .' It all depends what you mean by Christian. But tea is all they want and they go back to their ramble.

During the next creative session I go round trying to capture Christian's (Bunyan's Christian's) adventures on camera as they're rehearsed. The actors are undecided how to do the Gate scene and are experimenting with a white plastic clothes rack. Is there tension in the air? My heart beats uncomfortably as I remember moments of misery and confusion in other Quaker theatrical events. Loving-kindness sits uneasily with theatre. Theatre's a knockabout and fiery place; you need temperament, you need passion, you need authority, you need anger. Individually, Quakers get as angry as anyone, but corporately they're often no good at handling it. It's the same with authority. Having abandoned hierarchy, we get totally stuck in situations that simply need someone to say, 'That's enough talk. We ought to do it *this* way.'

Ten-year-old Eluned, one of the orgiasts at Vanity Fair, is garbed in a stringy black wig, a slinky black dress and loads of lipstick. She's Welsh/English bilingual like many others here. Her father can recite the most beautiful poetry in Welsh, and I can feel the religious tone of it even though I understand only the occasional word, like a Catholic at Latin Mass.

'Let's have a run-through,' says Gillian, at the piano. The play begins of course with us all singing 'He who would valiant be'. The adults, products of an era when Assembly meant Hymn Practice, know it well; some of the children don't know it at all, or any hymns. How I've loved and fought with the language of hymns! Take this one, which for me was 'Who would true valour see'. I love the notion of Pilgrim, the picture of a lone sturdy individual stalwartly striding along the stony path towards the brilliant goal. But as a child I knew that if I were Pilgrim, hobgoblins and foul fiends would rush down Lake District mountainsides towards me brandishing daggers and croaking obscenities. I can see the beastly little monsters even now. And lurking in a cave in the valley lived the massive-muscled, splay-footed, warty giant with whom I, sheepish little runt of a Pilgrim, would have to grapple if I was to prove my worth and enter the Celestial City.

Were those monstrous visions conducive to my spiritual health and development? Were they a Grimm fairy-tale that took up my nameless fears and gave them a bodily form which, however grotesque, made them easier for me to tackle? Were they a stage I had to go through, a pre-abstract realisation of the forces of good and evil I would face in the world? Or a load of medieval nonsense I would have been better off without?

It's always the music that gets me. As Doreen, playing Bunyan, lies down to sleep murmuring, 'The Lord is My Shepherd', Siobhan's sweet voice takes up Brother James' Air: 'The Lord's my Shepherd, I'll not want, He makes me down to lie In pastures green . . .' And I remember how it used to go in my childhood: 'God will lead me and comfort me. Be near me, Lord Jesus, I ask Thee to stay Close by me forever. Underneath are the everlasting arms.'

I'll never forget the sense of liberated loss I felt at the moment when I knew for sure that these feelings – the closeness of a powerful God who took special care of me – weren't with me any more. I was driving through town on Christmas Eve at three in the afternoon, and I casually switched on the radio to see if there was anything I might like to listen to. A clear high voice rang out in the confines of my little Nissan Micra: 'Once in royal David's city . . .' It was the Nine Lessons and Carols from King's College Chapel,

Cambridge, and for the first time in all my conscious years
I'd forgotten all about it.

I wander back to the scenery-makers and find that the
Celestial City is almost finished. The only remaining decision
is whether to put the clouds above or below the painted city.
We try fixing them below, but that makes the clouds look
like odd-shaped rocks. The Celestial City is supposed to be
'above the clear blue sky' – but no one, hardly anyone,
believes in heaven any more. We can't imagine it. We know
what's above the clear blue sky now: the visited moon, the
photographed Venus and Mars, a universe of light years and
black holes with Red Dwarf chugging through it and Arthur
Dent and Ford Prefect hitch-hiking.

There's an odd disjunction here. Religion is redolent with
metaphors of finite space and time, while it's the scientists
who are talking about infinity. 'Do you believe in God?' is
still posed as an either/or question, while even a lay science-
reader accepts that waves and particles behave like both particles and waves.

6 p.m. The evening meal brings Double Chocolate Fudge
Cake. I'm sitting with the young hobgoblins, who are per-
suaded not to squirt the ketchup into each other's faces and
now become transmogrified into solid, silent chocoholics.
Pete, the one who's been bothered about the meaning of
life, seems not bothered by it at the moment. I know that
he fights mercilessly with his younger brother and plays the
violin like a dream. What will he become? A footballer, a
jazz musician, a burger-maker, a parson, a computer hack?

I join a table of adults for coffee and we discuss politics.
What's to be done, asks Frank, with a Prime Minister who
says we must condemn more and understand less? Nearer
home, what about making a 'Greenway' – bus, cycle and
walkway – from the defunct railway line behind Annabel's
house? We agree that the politicians will use 'public consul-
tation' as a pretext for doing whatever they want. Political
language is language as cover, as front, as disguise for the real
power game. Same with religion?

Then we gather again in the Round Room for the evening's entertainment. Fifteen items are offered, from Paul's

creation of a poem out of an *Index of First Lines* – remarkably evocative, if meaningless – and Dave's rendering of *Hamlet* in multi-syllabic doggerel, to Megan's cello-playing and Siobhan's own-composed rock ballad. In the middle of the evening someone recites Leigh Hunt's 'Abu ben Adhem'. 'Write me as one who loves his fellow men', ben Adhem instructs the angel, in opposition to the command to love the Lord his God. And this was acceptable. Abu came top of the list of the saved. Yet Laurie was telling me last night over the meal table that when she was brought up in an evangelical Christian community she felt herself to be at the bottom of her parents' priority list. God came first, the world-in-need-of-saving next, the children last.

Who is this God who produces children and then abandons them? I've been asking that question since my first term at the boarding school, as I wiped the tears of my friend on the night her family sailed for India. That was the beginning of it, I think: the first time I wondered if God knew what he was doing . . . if God's word was in fact God's Word . . . if the Call was God's call . . . if God.

9 p.m. The evening ends with circle-dancing and cocoa. Someone has brought some Taizé music on tape: *Adoramus Te, adoramus te.* The steps are easy enough even for me, and I don't stop to wonder who I am adoring and whether the *Te* should have a capital letter or not. It's like the blissful moment when I came into my first Quaker meeting twenty-seven years ago and realised I needn't ask myself these frenetic questions about God and Jesus any more. I can just dance.

I'm at the end of the queue for drinks. I notice the accent of the woman on the staff who's serving cocoa and ask her where she comes from. She says Australia, but she hardly ever goes back there because she's frightened of flying. She used to be an air stewardess and knows the dangers. Suddenly we're talking very deeply about fear. 'We know we're in the Lord's hands, of course,' she says, but she's still afraid. I'm full of fears, not of flying, which I adore to the extent of thinking 'What a wonderful way to go', but that one of my children should die, or that I'll become senile, babbling and dribbly. Having no Lord to look after me I try to let my fears go, or face them first and then let them go; or just face them, visualise them, live in them, embrace the lions like Daniel in his den and hope they won't maul me to death. Again I think of *Elijah*: 'For He shall give His angels charge over thee'. This woman knows and sees God's angels, but she's still afraid. I don't know or see them, and I'm still afraid.

She doesn't know what I'm thinking, but we seem to have a sudden communion in our fears. Nothing is expressed in words, because we don't know each other well enough, and there's always the possibility that I might be kidding myself. But I know in my heart with a small insistent knowing that she and I have understood each other. It's a small instance when I have to trust myself without the reassurance of words.

I crawl into bed thinking, 'I love these people'. It's a tiny world, this little community, and it doesn't in any way serve as a prototype for the wider world. But it's a practice ground for loving. It has wonderful surprises and failed expectations and sudden insights and tense conflicts. It gives me the time and space to find out what loving is possible, and a fragile web of trust for my untrusting soul. If the web breaks, I panic and rush back into my self-protective shell of words until I can step out again into the silence.

3

THE GIRL IN THE BATHROOM SINGING

I enquired innocently [of the serpent], 'Why should I do what you want?' setting my mouth to the ribbed and purple fruit ... Yet at that precise moment, even as I laughed at him, drawing nearer to him again, as he perceptibly recoiled, my teeth began puncturing the skin of the fig. A childish, accidental act, you could say, this eating, in its beginning. Yet the moment that I realised what I did it became a knowledgeable bite, the considered, careful action of a woman who needing, as a woman, what the garden could not give her, had to take the risk that her husband would not follow ... I thought how sweet the fruit tasted and how strange, and only when I'd swallowed its last threads, its final seeds, started to wonder about tomorrow.

(PENELOPE FARMER, *Eve, Her Story*[1])

A friend who is a specialist in spiritual autobiography tells me that, in workshops, she asks people simply to write for five minutes starting with the words *I was born*. I recently went to a conference in Edinburgh with a group of fellow children's book enthusiasts and on Waverley Station I told them, 'I was born *here*.'

Released finally from my Yorkshire Methodist prison, I went to university. I'd chosen Edinburgh because of its great physical beauty, and because it was a busy city where I'd be challenged by urban realities rather than living on a quiet campus that would protect me from everyone except students and intellectuals. Such calm and courageous analysis from an immature seventeen-year-old – but inside I was consumed with excitement and terror. Real life had just begun.

Before I went, I knelt down by my bed and prayed that during these four years in Edinburgh I would learn to grow into a better person. I decided that this was what God wanted from me. It was what *I* wanted from me. Which? Or both? How can we ever know? By coincidences working out, perhaps? But don't we just notice the coincidences that do work out, and not notice the ones that don't? As I do with astrological forecasts – take note of those that fit what I want, dismiss the rest as rubbish.

In Edinburgh I made straight for the nearest religious institution and found exactly what I wanted: a mixture of safety and challenge. The theological college had set up a Christian Mission in one of the poorest parts of the city. Volunteers were needed to visit people, by invitation, in their 'single ends' – rooms in which whole families lived with the benefit of one cold tap – and to run out-of-school clubs for children. I had no qualifications for this sort of thing beyond what any Lady Bountiful has to offer: the experience of privilege, which confers the right to counsel the less fortunate on how to run their lives.

We were advised by the theology students that when visiting these dark, damp, high-ceilinged rooms we should say prayers with the residents. My companion Marion and I agreed that we didn't feel comfortable with spoken Christian prayer, especially when we didn't know anything about the religious belief of the people we visited or the ways in which they might naturally express it. I think we were stunned, too, by the contrast between the comfort of our lives, temporarily poor as we were, and the ingrained discomfort of the lives we were witnessing. At the top of the house lived a young woman with several small children and another on the way, and we used to watch her as she washed the family's clothes by hand in water that must have put as much dirt back in as it took out. One man, who lived on the first floor up, had had both legs amputated because of gangrene following minor injuries. He'd been granted a three-wheeled invalid car to get around in, which allowed no passenger/companion/carer, and when he arrived home he'd heave himself out of the car on his bum, lever himself on great muscular arms across the pavement and painfully groan his way up the gloomy stone stairway to his door. He looked after himself entirely. Another single end, which we weren't asked to visit, was obviously a brothel.

I felt as if I came from a different planet, and it must have seemed the same to the people I visited. If they wondered what we were hoping for they never indicated it. They welcomed us and gave us cups of hot sweet tea or Camp coffee with evaporated milk. Sometimes, pausing in the stairway, Marion and I would look at each other and ask, in our helpless mutual glance, what we were doing there at all. I told myself it was training for the greater work I would undertake: social work among the poor in London or some other bustling and terrifying city. I can't think why some older, wiser person didn't take me on one side and give me an insight into the politics of what I was doing. But this was the early '60s, before political consciousness had been raised, when people – certainly people of my class and background – really believed that ignorant women indulging in good works were simply wonderful.

Religion versus sex

The leaders of the Mission were young men in the later years of their theological training. I think I was in love with half of them most of the time, and sometimes one of them, usually a lonely overseas student, was in love with me. I knelt down beside my bed every night and asked God what I should do about these relationships and feelings. I was reading the whole of the Bible, too, a chapter a night, but, moving about between the books of the Bible to find the more interesting bits, I never conquered Ecclesiastes.

Sex and religion were constantly getting confused in my mind; the conjunction and disjunction between these two has been a source of fascination throughout my personal and professional life. If my love-life was going well and I felt good about it, I'd experience a great whoosh of religious enlightenment and gratitude to God, or if it was going badly and I felt deprived, I'd fall on my knees and pray that this inappropriate emotion should become God-directed and made pure. Toni Morrison's Pauline in *The Bluest Eye* felt the same confusion: 'There was a woman [in the church] named Ivy who seemed to hold in her mouth all of the sounds of Pauline's soul. Standing a little apart from the choir, Ivy sang the dark sweetness Pauline could not name; she sang the death-defying death Pauline yearned for; she sang of the Stranger who *knew* . . . Thus it was that when the Stranger, the someone, did appear out of nowhere, Pauline was grateful but not surprised. He came, strutting right out of a Kentucky sun on the hottest day of the year. He came big, he came strong, he came with yellow eyes, flaring nostrils, and he came with his own music.'[2]

I see that I was using a religious framework to express my sexuality because, coming from my sort of background, the religious format came most easily to me as I struggled to cope with the intensity of my feelings. Later, when insight began to dawn, I would look back and say, 'I thought it was religion, but actually it was only sex.' Now I think that's too dismissive, but it's a view that still has wide currency.

Most of my time at the Mission I felt like a nervous outsider. I was English in a very Scottish place, an Anglican/Methodist among Presbyterians, a private restless questioner among people who seemed sure of God and their relationship with Him. But they gave me a practical job to do and against all the odds I was good at it. First I helped with the after-school children's clubs and then I began to run them. I got to know wee Hughie (pronounced Shooey) with the endlessly running nose, tough red-haired Johnny who'd nick the toys soon as look at them, and Janet who was always at my side to help. I was disconcerted to find that I liked Johnny better than I liked Janet, though Janet was virtuous and a church-goer and Johnny was neither.

My favourite occasion in the Mission House, a ground-floor flat with a bright red door where four theology students lived and any of the volunteers were welcome any time, was the communion meal. We said no ritual words but sat round a simple table laid with bread and drinks, and mostly in silence took part in a communion, a fellowship, and felt a kinship in our shared work. Here was something real. It came in hurtful contrast to the devastating lack I felt on Sundays at the church communion table, where what was supposed to bring me the gift of the Holy Spirit brought merely a nothing, an emptiness.

This simple shared meal gave me a hint of what was to become so valuable later: a letting go of God-language while love with a spiritual base could develop in its own way. 'When I dreamt about you the other night, I felt that I joined you: I felt channels strengthening and opening up, and it was important that I told you about it. I want to reflect it back, make waves, an interference pattern. Perhaps something in what I say will validate for you what you are doing... I sometimes overflow with praise and thanks and it's embarrassing because I've nothing to attach it to, address it to. I rejoice in the pattern, in the dance. I'm occasionally caught up in joy and love and laughter and delight. There is limitless love in it, for me, and yet it's not personified at all.'[3]

In the rest of my free time I joined two student organisations, DramSoc and the Christian Union. Anyone could have told me that these two would pull me in different directions – that if the Christian Union gave me religion and forbade me sex, then the University Dramatic Society would offer me lots of unholy sex. And so it was. Students who were light years ahead of me in maturity, among them several confident Americans, strode the stage declaiming lines from Pinter and Jean Genet, and in the coffee breaks they'd use words like 'come' in ways I didn't understand.

Before the first term was out I'd decided that sex and drama were too bewildering, too dangerous. I'd stick for the moment with religion. Like the hero of Brian Patten's poem 'Ode on Celestial Music', I would do my best to ignore the bright flowers of sexuality that were pushing their way up through the floorboards:

> It's not celestial music it's the girl in the bathroom singing.
> You can tell. Although it's winter
> the trees outside her window have grown leaves,
> all manner of flowers push up through the floorboards.
> I think – what a filthy trick that is to play on me,
> I snip them with my scissors shouting
> '*I want only bona fide celestial music!*'[4]

But the Christian Union didn't offer mere religion. It offered a whole way of life. I joined CU because I'd met a kindly evangelical girl in one of the endless queues that greet 'freshers' during their first week and she invited me along. I needed kindness like I needed food – dry haggis and wet turnip in the Refectory, I remember.

The first thing I learnt from CU was that, if you'd got God properly, then sex was not forbidden, it was just unnecessary. Anne, the kind evangelical, had a man in the offing whom God had chosen as her husband, though she disliked him, and she knew in any case – perhaps fortunately, in her circumstances – that kissing was against God's law until after you were engaged. I had cause to be grateful for her kindness, which stretched far beyond the bounds of Christian duty and even into the sexual arena. One night, after midnight, when I was anguished because one of the theological students had stood me up, Anne met me in Princes Street and walked me up and down under a balmy summer moon until her prayerful sweetness had calmed my tears.

Round about this time I read Virginia Woolf's *To the Lighthouse*. One particular message made me ponder my confusion between sex and religion. 'Sitting on the floor with her arms round Mrs Ramsay's knees, close as she could get, smiling to think that Mrs Ramsay would never know the reason of that pressure, she imagined ... the chambers of the mind and heart of the woman ... What art was there, known to love or cunning, by which one pressed through into those secret chambers? What device for becoming, like waters poured into one jar, inextricably the same, one with the object one adored? Could the body achieve it, or the mind, subtly mingling in the intricate passages of the brain? or the heart? Could loving, as people called it, make her and Mrs Ramsay one?'[5]

What device for becoming, like waters poured into one jar, inextricably the same, one with the object one adored? Perhaps here, in this insight, lay the key to why Religion saw Sexuality as such a profound threat. For Religion says that it is God whom we should adore, God with whom we should long to be united. He alone should be the jar into which our loving waters are poured. In a powerful sexual relationship we adore and long for unity with a mere creature, a human being. Iris Murdoch puts it in a sentence: 'The absolute yearning of one human body for another particular one and its indifference to substitutes is one of life's major mysteries.'[6] The quotation goes on later: 'I felt no need to take control. It was not that Julian controlled me. We were both of us controlled by something else.' *Controlled by something else*: by the power of a complete relationship of body and spirit together – which may or may not endure, which may be based on sentimental illusion or personal need, but which at the time demands a preoccupation and a dedication that God would naturally resent. The Judaeo-Christian God is said to be a jealous God; those in His church whose duty is to lay down moral guidelines and maintain the social order can only condemn such devotion merely to a human being. But we have bodies as well as souls. I knew from my philosophy lectures that, ever since Darwin published his *Origin of Species*, theologians had been struggling with the 'Apes and Angels' debate and having difficulty reconciling themselves to the fact that human beings are both. It seems to me now, reflecting on my conflict then and still, that while we exist in this phase between birth and death, our bodies have needs and appetites, and at the same time our souls reach out for reciprocation. We have evolved as a species with our sexuality as a driving force, a force for life and love and continuation and purpose. But what is my life, what is its continuation and purpose, if not spirituality? How are these two purposes to be squared?

Ever since the break in my life at the age of eight, if not before, I longed for unity. That longing took two forms: the longing for unity with God and the longing for unity with another human being. I sensed that I might, in longing for unity with the source of myself and of all the world, achieve some approximation of that unity in a physical relationship with another human being. But I still hoped for unity with a Godhead who had yet to visit me.

Conversion

I learnt at the Christian Union that their God was indeed jealous. Not only was He against sex; He demanded that the CU reject all invitations from the Student Christian Movement to hold joint prayer meetings. As Anne explained, how could we possibly share our prayers with people who didn't believe the same as we did, i.e. The Truth?

It didn't take me long to realise that I couldn't stand this. They were expansive in their kindness, the whole gang of them, and they provided wonderful safety for an immature girl straight up from boarding school in England. But they were unbearably *certain*. When I asked them why a loving God should demand the blood of His Only Son before he could set about forgiving the sins of the whole world, they told me to have faith and not ask so many questions. When pushed they talked about Justice, which in my book came well down the priority list from Love. I seemed even at that stage to have no doubt at all that Love was the chief characteristic of the Divine.

I began to bring my studies in psychology into the discussions, arguing that if we were sinful because our parents had treated us badly when we were children, this was hardly a cause for self-abasement, or for redemption through some repellent blood sacrifice on the part of a long-ago, good, and by all accounts naturally forgiving man.

The other problem for me was the Christian Union members' insistence on the necessity for a conversion experience. This seemed to me like saying how vital it was to be struck by lightning. How could I ensure that it would happen? What would become of me if it didn't? If God wanted me to experience the ecstasy of conversion, wouldn't He arrange it? If He didn't, surely that wasn't my fault? But if it was my fault, what punishment or rejection awaited me? And why?

This relentless questioning reached a peak when I went to St Giles Cathedral to hear a sermon by an eminent scientist and Christian. Here surely would be the answer from a man with a top-class scientific brain. He could tell me the facts behind God and His demands; he would make it clear that it was me who was muddle-headed, not God Himself.

But no. From up in the organ loft, where I was allowed to sit during services because I was an organ pupil, I heard this brilliant scientist too enunciate the absolute necessity for receiving a bolt from the divine blue.

The finality of this message didn't actually depress or alarm me. It felt like a quiet release. Obviously, I thought, I wasn't the sort of person who should stand outside in spiritual thunderstorms. I didn't know where I should be standing, but obviously it wasn't here.

I stopped going to meetings of the Christian Union and stuck with the staid Presbyterian chapel in the middle-class half of the parish where the Mission operated. As with Methodism, the services lacked the evocative language of the Anglican Matins and Evensong. I can still come out in goose-pimples on hearing, 'We do not presume to come to this Thy table, O Lord, trusting in our own righteousness, but in Thy manifold and great mercies.' *Manifold and great mercies!* Who could resist them? But in the Presbyterian church there was the glory of the metrical psalms, and outside it I sang in many of the great oratorios in the university choir. I once even preached from the pulpit of the Mission church on the subject of 'giving these children of the dark streets the brightest light we know'. How did I *dare*? It makes me shudder to remember it. I suppose no one told me not to be so bloody arrogant because they were bloody arrogant themselves.

There are times, even now, when I'm talking to people I think of as 'real' believers – those whose beliefs, though traditional in form, have been won through personal search and at personal cost – when I suddenly think, 'I'm missing the point'. Their point, so far as I can grasp it, is that the Divinity takes a passionate interest in creation, sometimes in a particular part of it and in a particular human being, group or nation. God endows these people with a particular spirituality, which is their burden and privilege and which reveals itself in ministry or prophecy. They can reject the gift, or twist it, or wrestle with it. But if it is accepted and properly used it brings the Divine essence into people's lives. Grasped like this it is a wonderful belief, resonant with power.

But always, for me, it's the concept of power that separates me from it. Its underlying assumption is that *some* receive the gift, *some* are called. When I was researching the concept of ordination for my play *Heretics*, I heard the ordained ministry described as 'an exclusive club'. It reminded me of the exclusive club of the Christian Union at Edinburgh University. The place where I stand now, and was beginning to stand then, is where there are no exclusive clubs: where every individual, group or nation can draw on their own spiritual resources and be empowered to grow spiritually in their own way while respecting the ways of others. Sheila Rowbotham again: 'Then came the realisation that we needed to resist not only the outer folds of power structures, but their inner coils. For their hold over our lives through symbol, myth and archetype would not dissolve automatically with the other bondages even in the fierce heat of revolution. There had to be an inner psychological and spiritual context along with the confrontation and transformation of external powers.'[7]

The key to the faith of many of those who stay in the mainstream of the Christian church is their experience of *communion*. That's what I looked for in what proved, for me, to be an empty sacrament, and what I'd found in the shared meal with the Mission students. I tried again, later in my university days, when I went regularly with a friend to the 8 a.m. communion service at the Episcopal Church of Scotland, which is part of the Anglican church. My friend Jan was my landlady, a doctor with children of my age, a sharp sense of humour, and an even sharper sense of morality and good sense. She was a wonderful companion at this stage of my life and at this time in the affairs of the nation. The Profumo affair was in full swing. On a Sunday she and I would swig an early cup of tea, drive down to the church to kneel and receive our sacrament, then drive back and stop off at the baker's to buy warm Scottish baps and at the newsagents for the *Sunday Times* and the *News of the World*. Then we'd race home to read the latest scandal and gaze at Christine Keeler leaning naked over her upright wooden chair. I was gleefully aware of the leap we were making in that half-hour, and glad to be with someone who took it for granted we could make the leap with impunity.

It was when I was living in Morningside with Jan that I experienced the near-death of the world during the Cuba crisis. I clearly remember, as everyone does, the place where I heard the news of the death of President Kennedy. But I remember even more keenly where I stood, outside the university refectory in Edinburgh, clutching hold of my friend Margaret, with each of us hugging the other in shaking terror as we realised that the world might end at any moment in nuclear holocaust.

It didn't occur to me that God would save the world from disaster. There was nothing in the language I'd heard in any church to cover these circumstances. In fact few of the people I'd met within any church discussed politics at all, and I knew that Leonard Cheshire, who had inspired my parents to help set up one of his Homes for the chronic sick, was both deeply religious and in favour of the nuclear deterrent. Margaret, with whom I shared the realisation and the terror, was a church-goer too, but first and last she was politically aware, a young woman who had learned her politics the hard way by coming into higher education every day by bus from her council estate home on the outskirts of the city. She had taught me about class structures, and she'd drummed into me, by her actions as much as her arguments, about human beings taking responsibility for the consequences of their actions. Some of my friends might have thought that God would save the world from its own folly, but I knew deep inside that this nuclear folly was for us and only us – governments and citizens alike – to sort out.

Around the same time, at home with my family, there raged unholy arguments about the latest writing of John Robinson,

Bishop of Woolwich. *Honest to God* was just published and had set church and nation in a frenzy. What did he mean, 'God is the Ground of our Being'? What was the church coming to, being so philosophical; shouldn't it be preaching the gospel to the simple faithful? It was all very well for academics to speculate like this, but the man was a *bishop*!

I didn't understand what was going on here, either within my family or in the world of the theologians. I could see, in front of my eyes, that there was more to this than a dispute about Higher Beings. I could feel the personal passions that were wrapped up inside theological argument. Here was theology being used as a weapon instead of a refuge, a highly potent stimulant instead of a balm. But I had no idea what my own theological stand was. I had no true experience of who God was, or what was the role of God – my sort of God or anyone else's – in the world I had begun to explore. There were so many *Don't knows* in my answers to the Christian questionnaire. What was the point of my filling it in at all?

Outside Christianity

By this time the sex part had sorted itself out for the moment in the shape of a young man who wasn't a theological student but a practical, down-to-earth student of social work. That was the field I had chosen for myself, and things were going very well. It was time for a foray into more exotic areas of the spiritual life. Through another branch of good works I met a small group of Baha'is, and learnt about their faith.

Looking up 'Baha'i' in the encyclopaedia told me that it was an off-shoot of Islam. But the Baha'is I met didn't describe themselves in that way and there seemed little except cultural aspects that was Islamic in what I found. The two of the faithful I got to know best were called Eric and Paul, and I know that Eric at least has gone on to overseas work in the cause – yes, missionary work, but taking his family with him. They were an interesting pair, refreshingly open-minded after the claustrophobia of the Christian Union. Baha'is, they told me, believed in World Government; in there being no division between science, religion and the arts; that there should be no discrimination between men and women; and, best of all, that the religions of the world were all part of a process of the gradual revelation of God. Their own prophet Baha'u'llah, and his son and successor Abdul Baha, preached that God shows just as much of himself and in just such a way as human beings can absorb at any one time.

Paul and Eric were fun to be with. Paul had just come back from two years in Lapland where he'd lived like a Laplander and spoken about the Baha'i faith to anyone who wanted to hear. I learnt that many Baha'is did this stint of two years' missionary work, but they were discouraged from aggressive proselytising, and their attitude to me and the others in the circle bore out this gentle approach. Eric smoked revolting herbal tobacco in a flimsy pipe, and we played endless games of bad bridge.

Eric was engaged to a young woman whose father was an elder of the local kirk, and it was through this circumstance that I learnt the more rigid aspects of Baha'i life – aspects which I've since realised probably come more from its cultural accretions than from the essence of the faith itself. It seemed that, at whatever age a couple wished to marry, they must always have the consent of their parents. Eric's own father was an English vicar. When each set of parents learnt of this convenient rule they set about alternating in their refusal of consent to the marriage, presumably in the hope that the young things would give up this crazy oriental religion and return to the Christian fold.

Looking more closely at the small print of the Baha'i faith, I discovered that there were quite a few of these regulations: a nineteen-day month, for instance, which made planning of weekends difficult. I realised that I was concentrating too much on trivialities when The Truth was at stake, but I couldn't cope. I couldn't cope with the cultural change, and for me the essence of culture lay in language. The language of Christianity flowed in my blood as it coursed through my brain. The language, the stories, the rules of another faith seemed . . . too foreign? Too much like hard work? Whichever way I look back, my attitude seems humblingly small-minded.

Eric and his fiancée finally managed to get both sets of parental consent for long enough to arrange their wedding, and I remember it vividly. First came the Presbyterian service in Greyfriars Kirk. Then we trooped, following the bride in her long white dress, over the zebra crossing to the Chaplaincy Centre, which was liberal enough even then to house a Baha'i wedding. The occasion was beautiful in an utterly oriental way: quiet and dignified and poetic. But it was alien to me. Most of the time, I'm ashamed to admit, I had my eyes fixed on the food that was laid out in the side aisle.

Eventually I told Eric that I was sorry but I would stick with Christianity for the moment until things became clearer. He said that was fine. He'd always told me that it didn't matter which religion you adhered to, because all religions were one. But our friendship lapsed.

I felt sad and cowardly, and then relieved, and then depressed at the thought of tackling the Christian churches once again to find something that suited me. What a fuss-pot I was. Why couldn't I accept what other people accepted, and say the confession and the creed like a good girl? Or else why couldn't I chuck religion in the dustbin like so many of my friends were doing and make hay while the '60s sun shone?

I suppose the twin answers to that last question were, on the one hand, that I knew I was profoundly religious/spiritual and could never give it up, and on the other that I was too scared. Religion gave me a lifeline and a safety net and, when I left Edinburgh to come south and be a Child Care Officer in the London Borough of Hackney, I needed them.

I've found a piece in my diary which gives an insight into my years in Edinburgh from that recent visit. I remembered my prayer that I should 'grow into a better person', and wrote: 'These few days have brought back to life those four years that were the rebirth of Ali as a personal and spiritual being. I didn't know what "a better person" might be. I just knew that I had to grow. My growth might need to be private, hidden from disapproving eyes because "they" wouldn't understand, but I knew that my spirit was wholesome, life-giving, good. It was *enough to go on*, literally: enough not to go round in circles or to stop – enough to be going on with, and to go forward.'

4

DISCOVERING MY OWN HEARTBEAT

> We human beings are all in the same difficulty. We are all torn asunder, *all of us*, by this disintegration of our flesh and spirit. And so if in this book I am appearing more spiritual than credible to some of those I have loved, let them examine their own consciences. I think they will discover, as I have done, that they also are torn asunder and that they also have desired to be made whole.
>
> (ERIC GILL[1])

Now I was off to London with another great purpose: to set up my brilliant career of doing good to suffering humanity. Only clichés will do. When I was asked by the interviewing panel of the London Borough of Hackney Children's Department, 'Why do you want to do this job?' I'd replied, 'I've been given so much, I want to give something back.' I had no idea what I was saying.

In both the job and the great purpose I was a total and almost immediate failure. Could this have been God's intention for me? I lasted eleven months. Those months involved personal terror fuelled by a sinking awareness of my ignorance of the world. I realised that my politics were based on a completely erroneous assumption of my superiority. It was my own power that terrified me, because I had no qualification for it except through the British class system. I didn't understand any of the lives – lives of people from St Kitts or Jamaica, lives of people described as ESN or subnormal, incestuous lives, chaotic and poverty-hardened lives – in which I was supposed to intervene as authoritative helper. I was asked to remove children from their homes where necessary, place them within the day in an alien world, and it depended on my energy and wisdom (and that of my supervisor, who had other people to supervise) whether that child was decently placed in a safe home or not.

After six months of tapping on doors hoping there would be no answer, and placing deprived children in foster, adoptive and children's homes on the basis of minimal acquaintance with the facts, I went down with a series of infections and started to apply for other jobs. My only comfort, looking back on this interval, is that those who employed me were marginally more culpable than I was myself, because they were more experienced than me and ought to have been more aware.

Again I turned for safety to the church, its choir, and its Youth Club where I was of course a helper, not an ordinary member. It was the local Anglican parish church. Even there I opted for some un-safety by going out with a man in the church who was fascinating, a brilliant musician, yet a compulsive liar and who, I gradually began to realise, was having an affair with an older man in the choir. He was probably trying out a relationship with me partly out of curiosity and partly for respectability, because this was before the 1967 law which decriminalised homosexual acts between consenting adults in private.

The vicar of the church was an ex-colonial who had joined the ministry in his fifties. He retained many of the attitudes of the colonial service, and this was the time of Iain Macleod's great unwinding of Empire. He used to have fights with the uppity young organist over hymn tunes: sometimes these fights were conducted during the actual singing of a hymn, with the vicar shouting one version or at one speed and the organist playing a different one, pedals only, all stops out, maximum volume. At the Youth Club I got to know two teenage brothers from British Honduras and felt the impact of their wish to be respected as British citizens, rather than patronised or despised as 'coloured immigrants'. I also made friends with some local lads who were keen to educate me out of the naïvity of my sexual assumptions.

One Sunday – it must have been in the autumn of 1965 – the vicar spoke on the Rhodesian Unilateral Declaration of Independence. He preached the necessity and moral correctness of Britain sending troops to Rhodesia to fight for 'our kith and kin', the whites.

In the midst of my confusion, here was an issue on which I suddenly knew where I stood. I knew, in terms of politics in its widest meaning, that I was on the opposite side from this powerful man in the pulpit. God was urging him to preach for white over black, for war over peace, for the West – or the North, as we might put it today – over Africa. Something in me protested that his God was wrong. I couldn't have articulated it like that, because my parents were politically conservative and empire-supporting and I hadn't yet thought through where I stood as a free-standing political individual. But, as I shook hands with the vicar on leaving the church, I spoke to him. I've no idea how I found the courage; I have an image of myself at the time as conventional and timid. I said, 'I'm afraid I completely disagree with you about fighting for our kith and kin in Rhodesia.'

If at this point he'd said, 'Come and see me, we must discuss this', he might have saved me for tradition and patriarchy. But then, he might not, because the essence of patriarchy is authority, and I'd questioned his authority. He was enraged, speechless. I walked away, shaking, leaving the issue wafting unresolved on the air. We never did discuss it, though he treated me afterwards with some respect, even welcoming my relationship with the gay musician as something that might 'do him good'.

Did God care for me?

I've recently asked myself at what point I began to doubt the existence of an outer, interventionist God, a God who cared for me, who might step into the world arena on my behalf. I think it was during this period that my experience began to direct me away from this sort of God.

At the end of the relationship with the musician, and feeling intense identification with some of the children I'd taken into care, I relived the pain of being abandoned when I was a child. For the first time, curled up in bed, hurting as I'd never allowed myself to hurt before, I knew in the depths of myself that the only imperative was to *stay there* – simply to go on hurting. I knew that nothing would take away the pain; that if I was alone, then I was alone, that even though some part of me hoped for, even trusted in, a sort of healing, it wasn't there for me now and wouldn't be there until the pain had been lived through. Though there might be light at the end of the tunnel, the essence of a tunnel is that there *is* no light, and – to use the Christian metaphor which, at the time, I couldn't find in the church that offered it to me – the crucifixion had to be endured, death taken as final, and resurrection unthinkable. Only after I'd truly stayed with the pain and rejection and abandonment and let it engulf me could there be the possibility of new life.

Time and again, when I look at my spiritual journey, I ask how my search is connected with the very different spiritual and political path of my parents, and my often painful relationship with the two of them. For them, as for most of their generation, 'spirituality' meant the Christian religion. It was simply a question of which church you went to. Other faiths were necessarily foreign and probably wrong. Meditation, transcendental or other, wasn't an option until the Beatles went to India, and even after that it was weird, fey, way out. Though we as a family knew about the Quakers because we'd lived in York, a city dominated by the Rowntree family who were Quakers, I'd always assumed you had to be born one. In any case they were impossibly good.

My parents seemed sure that their way was right. Yet I was different from them. Similarly, the church seemed sure that its way was right, and I was different from it. Where did that leave me? What did right – wrong – different – mean? Who or what was 'God', this Being who I was told cared for every hair on my head? And what if I felt He didn't, or even wasn't?

One central certainty was that every aspect of my life had been affected – coloured, twisted, focused, fraught – by the abrupt separation from home and family when I was eight. Did that give me my first inkling that God might not care? Perhaps. As a child and a young adult I prayed fervently every night. Maybe I didn't expect answers? Maybe I rejected the questions? I needed to have faith that my life was in safe hands: the hands of my parents, and of God. Yet those hands were not safe. At some level I knew that.

The move to boarding school had been presented to me and my ten-year-old sister, far from being a potential trauma, as a great excitement, a privilege. I accepted what my mother said about privilege and excitement, never doubting that she, like God, knew what was good for us. I thought we were going to Enid Blyton's Mallory Towers. None of Enid Blyton's merry characters hinted at the core boarding school emotions which are separation, rejection, alienation and bewilderment. So when I felt those things I thought it was me who was wrong or peculiar. I even thought I might be mistaken in thinking I felt them at all.

Why did our parents send us there? Obviously, for a good education. But would they not miss us? The question took on greater weight when we learnt that our father had himself been miserable at his prep school in Windermere where he was sent at the age of seven. It was always made clear to us that his parents, at any rate his mother, had not loved him like our parents loved us. So – *did* our parents love us?

This is a peculiarly English middle-class grinding-mill. I've met parents who sent their children to boarding school out of love, and their children agree that this is so. But many other children conclude that their parents cannot have loved them enough to keep them at home in a day-to-day relationship, and eventually I joined this band. What they said about loving me was not true or, at any rate, they didn't love the person I knew as me. But they continually told us they did love us, and this was the source of an even deeper bewilderment.

It's in response to this realisation that people say, 'Well, if they don't love me, then God will.' Was that what happened to me?

It's a complicated, foggy picture. When thinking about my early image of God I've written: 'What woman could say, *I am that I am*?' Yet my mother did say that. Her word, in our house, ruled. And *word* it was. She, the only one of her family to go into higher education, gained a First Class Honours degree in English and medals in each of her university years. She published two novels in her twenties. She knew how to use words powerfully. Our father adored her. He ministered to her frequent and in the end constant illnesses, and honoured her creative talent, though she didn't use it a great deal after she took on the role of wife and mother. So, apart from finding myself with a complex relationship with Father God, I'm also a fairly complex kind of feminist.

My mother gave me my love of language. But she also offered me her creed. She believed in the saving power of language: that if you could sum things up in a beautiful or resounding phrase it took on unquestionable power. I accepted this creed with my whole heart. She said we were happy at school. I believed her and denied the reality. The tension between creed and reality can last for so long; then it breaks down.

I think – I'm almost sure – that I talked to God before I went away to boarding school at eight. How far can you trust your memories? I thought I remembered scribbling stories right from my earliest years at school. Then I doubted. Then I checked with an old school friend and she confirmed that my memory was right. 'You scribbled all the time,' she said. 'I remember that story about the fox-cubs.' I remembered the story about the fox-cubs too. Yet some of my memories may not be reliable. During a deliberate remembering of childhood I found myself on York Station, on the platform nearest the barrier. My sister is seven and I am five, and Daddy – who, with Mother, cares for us like God cares for us – is looking around for a homely woman to keep an eye on us during the long journey ahead. Mother is ill, in hospital for a really serious operation, and we've got to go to London where we will be met by Auntie Margaret (whom we must have met on occasions, but don't know well enough to recognise) and we're going to have, because Mother has told us we will have, a lovely time. Crisis: there's no suitably homely woman available! Yes, there is . . . over there, sitting at a table in the carriage. . . .

But surely there weren't tables in the carriages then? I must have misremembered it. Yet I can see that homely woman in my memory and she's sitting on the other side of a table. I've reconstructed it wrong. She must have sat on a hard scratchy seat facing us, knee to knee.

Have I reconstructed God wrong, too?

The woman said yes, of course she'd look after us, and she did, she chatted to us all the way to London and I felt safe. . . . Looking back, I feel outrage that Daddy thought his place was with Mother, in hospital for her thyroid operation, rather than with us, two girls aged five and seven, alone on a train journey to London. He could have travelled there with us, handed us over to the unknown aunt, then travelled back. Did he have to stay with Mother? Did he have to go to work? I feel outrage – and yet when I first noted the memory I wrote, *I felt safe*.

Later I articulated the feeling: 'I don't think I ever fully trusted Daddy again after that.' But I may be inventing, building into the situation a feeling that actually came later. Trust: that feeling, which cannot be denied if it is there or manufactured if it is not, is the basis of faith in God. Yet, if I mistrusted my father for sending us on that journey, I went on trying to trust my mother and her creed for many years, and trying to trust God. I steadfastly believed that she had my best interests at heart because she said in such convincing language that she did.

At some point that belief, and all attempt at trust, disappeared. Then belief in a God who intervened to care also disappeared. Trust, if not in God, then in life, was something I had to rediscover, along with a fresh creed, fresh words, and even an ability to let words go.

I ask myself again: did this earlier separation spark off my talking with God? Must it be a particular experience of separation that I'm looking for to explain it? Does it need explaining in that way? Isn't the never-ending, existential human experience of separation, the terrifying awareness of human aloneness, in itself enough? I'm not looking to explain 'away' my tendency to explore everything within a spiritual framework, in a language of spirituality. But, if I can use for a moment the logician's way of examining a concept by looking at its negative, I find myself fascinated by people who have no religious leanings at all, and aren't inclined to take my way out by describing themselves as 'spiritual'. Their thinking seems so simple, so practical, so clear. My friend Jennifer, the one who had cancer, looked at some books I lent her on Quakerism and said, 'If I were religious, that sort of stuff would really appeal to me. But I'm not, so it doesn't.' She was ethical, political and philosophical in her thinking. She just wasn't religious or spiritual. She wasn't made that way. And that was that.

Why am I not like her?

Well, I'm not like her. I can ask 'Why?' till the desert freezes and the camels come skating home. I don't only *feel* I'm on a spiritual path, I *know* I'm on a spiritual path. As, in that breath-taking moment in his *Face to Face* interview with John Freeman, Carl Gustav Jung said, 'I don't *believe*.' (Pause.) 'I *know*.'

Yet at the same time I accepted Jennifer's position as valid for her. We couldn't have been friends if I didn't.

I know it would be tidy and convenient to conclude that I've been seeking all my life for a God who would fill the aching space created by my childhood deprivation. That may be part of the answer, but it doesn't seem to be the whole answer. I refused to accept the all-embracing God of the fundamentalists at university; in fact I've never been able to accept a faith that offered me answers. I've always wanted questions. I'm attracted to Eastern spirituality but I avoid anything that offers a guru. I don't want a father or a mother for a God. I want a friend – a partner – many friends, many partners – a goal – moving goal-posts, even. I want equality, dignity, mutual respect. I want to journey spiritually as an adult, not as a child.

A fascinating aspect of all this is that my sister, when we were children, reacted quite differently to our family and school circumstances, yet she now stands in a very similar place to the one where I stand. She never believed that God cared for her. I was once deeply shocked when she asserted as we walked round a park (I could take you to the very spot where she said it): 'I think God invented the Devil so He could have someone to blame all His mistakes on.' How could she be so blasphemous? Yet I was impressed. My sister was older than me; she always looked after me. Her opinion couldn't be dismissed. What she said even made sense.

Here were dangerous waters. I pushed them to one side, like pushing aside some kind of rolling Red Sea, dammed them firmly, and ploughed on over my stony ground. I was still ploughing and damming through my eleven months in Hackney. But questions of power and belief were pressing, at work, in the church, and when I visited Israel.

Israel – holy, holy and differently holy

It was my sister who invited me to Israel. While I was working in London she'd gone travelling and was now working on a kibbutz in the Galilee region. I was relatively rich: might I fly out for a couple of weeks?

A kibbutz! For years I'd felt the pull of that dream. During my first year at university I'd planned to go, even bought books to learn modern Hebrew, but had taken sensible advice and chickened out. My awareness of the Jewish experience had been powerfully coloured first by my parents' casually derogatory remarks about Jews, which puzzled me, and then by the literature of the war and the death camps, about which I will write more fully later. I was drawn to the holy places of Israel partly in reverence for the land where the Jesus of my childhood had walked and preached and died, partly in astonishment at the miracle of a territory where Jews from all over the world could gather together and live in egalitarian communities.

It was 1966, the year before the Six Day War. I was utterly unprepared for the impact of that tiny strip of embattled earth. We stayed some days on the kibbutz; then we travelled, youth hostelling, to the predominantly Arab town of Nazareth, to Haifa with its Baha'i Temple, and to the hot white pavements and the tightly-packed hills of Jerusalem.

In the kibbutz I couldn't decide whether I was impressed or outraged at the sight of a philosophy professor mucking out the chicken house. The kibbutz children spent so little time with their parents! Could this be emotionally sustaining? And the Jewish faith – I'd assumed it was the centre of everything in this country – but some of these Israelis seemed to be almost atheists! And there was an unbridgeable chasm between the short-term, mostly non-Jewish visiting workers whose attitudes ran the gamut from romantic to caustic, and the resident kibbutzniks.

We took a boat over the Sea of Galilee from Tiberias and ate fish – in an expensive restaurant, not on the rough biblical shore – at the other side. We walked the bare archaeological site that is Capernaum and, just as I was struggling to feel the presence of Jesus in the ancient stones, we were hailed by some loud Christians from the hostel who declared they'd stood on the actual spot where Jesus was tempted. In Jerusalem we marvelled at the Dead Sea Scrolls and the Chagall windows. Later, sick as dogs from the heat or some unwholesome food, we were cared for by monks in a cool hospice right beside the then border with the Arab enemy. Struggling on to the roof look-out as the sun set we could see the Dome of the Rock, one of the holy places of Islam, gleaming.

I felt then, and have felt many times since, that if I've lived other lives before this, one of them would have been as a Jew wandering with Moses towards the end of the time in the wilderness. As that young man or woman I might have looked with Moses and Joshua over to the land of Canaan, the land flowing with milk and honey, which the Lord God of Israel had promised should be ours. This person who is me and not-me might have murmured: 'But there are people living there already. Isn't the Lord God of Israel their God, too?'

Two moments stand out. One was the press of people in the centre of Jerusalem for the celebration of independence, when I had a glimpse of the vision that had brought me to Israel: of a gathering from many nations, a people who have suffered and come through, in security and gladness singing their songs together. While I felt alien from the hot-tempered fraughtness of this country, and fearful of the stories I'd been told about the stoning of women in the stricter areas of the city for being dressed as I dressed myself, yet at the same time I was awed at the oneness of these men and women – so long dispersed and unimaginably persecuted, who only two or three decades before and by the hand of so-called Christians had undergone the worst that humanity could inflict – now living here, together, Jewish, in their own land, under their own responsibility and control.

The other, in complete contrast, was the cool light of the Baha'i Shrine, with its pale green and white marble and its shining bare floors, which stands under a golden dome high on a hill in Haifa overlooking the Mediterranean. Here lay the remains of Abdul Baha. There was no hymn or sermon to celebrate him, no leaflet thrust into my hand informing me about Baha'u'llah or the tenets of the faith, no inscription demanding that I worship the God of the Baha'is or believe the words of his prophet. Simply, cool and quiet. I could hear the drawing of my own breath.

Yet I couldn't be a Baha'i. I hadn't been able to become one, didn't want to become one. Obviously I wasn't a Jew. I supposed I was a sort of Christian, though I couldn't say which sort. What language could I find that was my own?

Power

I came back from Israel to the east London church where the vicar declared that there was one religion, Christianity, and Anglicanism was its prophet. It felt claustrophobic and I was angry with him all the time. I didn't declare, 'This is too hierarchical; I cannot accept the Lord/servant metaphor for the spiritual life; I revolt against the scandal of Christian particularity and embrace a multi-faith scenario.' But I started asking the sort of questions that led me to see, underlying all Christian and indeed other religious institutions, a structure of worldly rather than spiritual power. What right had a vicar to promote his political opinions from his position six feet above contradiction? Who decided which individual, which gender, which nation, which faith, was the elect of God? By what chance or intent, and through what edifice of power, did one person's experience become absorbed into the life of the community as especially significant, as prototype, as myth?

I felt so weak and insignificant. Didn't everyone feel like that? Clearly not. Some people assumed – in both senses of that word – power. I'd assumed it myself. I had seen, in Hackney, that other people could be made weak by *my* exercise of power. I was tossed between holding undue power and feeling aghast at my essential impotence.

The natural reaction to impotence is to seize power for ourselves as soon as the opportunity offers, and I'd done just that. In hierarchical institutions it's a natural progression: the fag becomes prefect, the private becomes Regimental Sergeant Major. In life, the Czechoslovakian orphan displaced by war walks across Europe and becomes the media magnate Robert Maxwell. Having overcome impotence and gained power – as soldier, doctor, priest, man, insider of any sort, or simply as adult – we can then wield power in the same way as it was wielded over us. The pattern has been set, the script has been written; the only task is to change our role from the submissive to the dominant. Once we gain that power the last thing we want to acknowledge is the impotence that we've overcome. So the parent resists the child's defencelessness, the priest resists identifying with the faithful in the pews, the psychiatrist resists understanding the patient's pain. So it had happened to me: I'd leapt from being a powerless child to an adult taking power over the lives of powerless children. I'd done it with the highest of motives, but that didn't change the fact that I held a God-like power over those children's lives.

Why couldn't I spot the progression from submission to dominance as it was happening? I suppose it just comes naturally in the sequence of things. I thought what everybody thinks: 'I deserve it, don't I, after all I've been through?' I did spot it, years later, when I experienced the same transition in a different context. On that occasion I'd leapt from being a humble contributor to magazines, a supplicant collecting rejection slips and the occasional cheque, to being the editor of a small journal. When one contributor fiercely resisted my rejection of his article I caught myself thinking, 'How *dare* he? Who does he think he is? *I'm* the editor, *I'll* decide!'

There is an alternative to glorying in power, and that is to glory in subjection. I'd experienced that reaction, too, especially in my position as a woman in relation to men, and especially in the church. I was only too ready to take the word of the man in a relationship as truth, and of the man in the pulpit as gospel. Subjection seems a natural form for women in the Christian life, where men have traditionally defined women in terms of impurity, and suffering is ordained by the God who knows better than we do what's good for us. There were plenty of role models for me in history and in the church pews. On the other hand I could read Simone Weil, who would show me how to move from ritual subjection to personal power: from words like, 'The duty of acceptance in all that concerns the will of God, whatever it may be, was impressed upon my mind as the first and most necessary of all duties' to 'The conviction was suddenly borne in upon me that Christianity is pre-eminently the religion of slaves.'[2] Was I a slave, or was I a slave-driver? Where lay some sort of personal power that wouldn't involve crushing other people?

The question became more urgent as I saw some of my foster and adoptive placements breaking down. I'd sent a small black Catholic boy to a lovely family in the Home Counties; too late it dawned on me that they'd become foster parents to assuage their guilt at using contraception, and his testing behaviour was too heavy a burden for such a flimsy motive. There was a brother and sister I was especially fond of, and I'd been so happy to find a distant aunt and uncle to care for them. But the relatives hadn't been able to cope and the pair were now thrown back into the cavernous dormitories of the Assessment Centre. My power had been compounded by ignorance, and I was ashamed.

Belief structures and personal perception

As I struggled with the language of religious belief, the feeling grew in me that power structures and belief structures are dependent on each other. A belief, when it is defined and set down as a formula, becomes externalised into a creed. It must have originated as a spontaneous, inward perception, but because that perception wasn't owned by its perceiver as personal and mutable, it hardened into something 'out there', 'objective'. In this way orthodoxies are established, heresies defined and heretics disowned; at the very least, if we as individuals disagree with the authorities we are marked as 'unsound'.

From a later perspective I can see this more clearly. *My perceptions are the only thing I know.* It seems almost banal to say such a thing, but I doubt it all the time and rush to other people – in books, in history, in dogma – for confirmation of what I might know or to ask how I can interpret my tiny morsel of life's precious gift in someone else's terms. I back up my perceptions by quoting St Augustine or St Paul. But St Augustine's experiences were internal, unique to him; so were Thomas Aquinas', Origen's, Kierkegaard's, St Paul's. The experiences were indisputable to them as individuals at that moment, just as my experiences are indisputable to me at the moment when they overtake me. They are what they are, no less and no more.

I began to wonder how my life would be if I could truly own my spiritual experience – claim it, reclaim it, value it, honour it; if I could know for certain that though people might say, 'I think you're mistaken in the value you place on your experience' or 'My experience is different', they could never truthfully say, 'That experience has no value' or 'You didn't experience that'. Then my unspoken longings wouldn't remain silent, or my vision be clouded. My words and my vision would stir in their spiritual womb, and I would see that they were in one sense unique, but at the same time they were linked with all other words and visions and longings that there had ever been.

I wasn't in outward crisis. But I knew the old order wouldn't suffice any longer. Security within the church, instead of being safety, had become a prison. I'd been numb in my spiritual life since the break with the Baha'is. The numbness now began to itch like a gone-to-sleep arm: painful, but in a liberating way. I longed for the loosening of assumptions, for a sudden awareness that would show me a world a thousand times as big and with a million more wonders than I'd ever imagined. There's a passage in Toni Morrison's *Beloved* that expresses in heightened form what I was longing for. A woman is describing her first sense of freedom from slavery: 'Something's the matter. What's the matter? . . . Suddenly she saw her hands and thought with a clarity as simple as it was dazzling, "These hands belong to me. These *my* hands." Next she felt a knocking in her chest and discovered something else new: her own heartbeat. Had it been there all along? This pounding thing? She felt like a fool and began to laugh out loud.'[3]

I wanted to dedicate myself to a spiritual life, but the only way

I knew to do it as a woman was to become a vicar's wife or a nun. Nothing was surer than that I couldn't go down the road to a cloistered existence, and the men I'd gone out with since working at the Edinburgh Mission were not clergy. Anyway, I didn't want to be a vicar's wife.

In order to own what my spirit was, I had to step out of the power structure of the church. But how? I didn't know.

I had internalised the hierarchy. I didn't know how to throw it off. I yearned for the act of liberation that would lead to a new kind of reality. Not a safe reality, in fact a terrifying one; not reliable, in fact exhausting, because each move had to be rethought afresh; but exhilarating, real. I'd read about Shaw's St Joan when she chose to burn at the stake rather than live incarcerated in gaol: 'Give me that writing. [*She rushes to the table; snatches up the paper; and tears it into fragments*] Light your fire: do you think I dread it as much as the life of a rat in a hole? My voices were right!'[4] But my courage, like my situation, isn't like St Joan's. My courage has always been of the two-steps-forward, one-step-back kind: mostly confusing, with sparks of light and occasional suffusing warmth. Most of the gains have been through the love of other people, and through being given support when I've needed it to overcome the fear that Power would overwhelm me, that I might be annihilated, that I had no right to exist in the first place.

The key seemed to lie in being true to myself. But I had no idea who that self was.

Two things happened to give me clues. I began applying for jobs, and for a place on courses that would further my social work career. In the end I had two options: to do a year's intensive course in London which would make me into a high-level professional with good prospects for future promotion, or to take up a post in Yorkshire at a salary lower than the one I was currently earning in a gentle, undynamic department well to one side of mainstream social work. How to decide? On either side of a blank postcard I wrote down the pros and cons of each. Then I assessed the results. Clearly I should accept the place on the professional course in London.

But I didn't want to. My intuition said, 'Step sideways, step north.' I obeyed my intuition and prepared to move.

Having made the decision to go, it seemed a good idea to have another fling with the brilliant musician. He was more at ease, too, having gained a place as a mature student to study music at Cambridge. He told me about his spiritual journey – in the first stage of our relationship I'd had no idea he was even *on* a spiritual journey – and he gave me a copy of a book which he said had changed his life. It was H. A. Williams' *The True Wilderness*. I read it and found words about true power being the strength that comes from wholeness within. What was needed to gain this power was quite simple: 'More light, deeper perception, a less clouded vision of what life is about. How am I to get it? Only in the ancient school of experience, by trial and error, by pain and joy, and, most of all, by faith, by confidence that, in spite of all appearances to the contrary, life is on my side and not against me.'[5]

The word 'faith' translated itself to me as 'trust', and it stirred something like music inside me. It sang the same song as the impulse to get a less powerful job, to live in a new city and try out new relationships.

I'd begun to realise that the God I'd been offered didn't exist for me, but that the human being who was me did exist and was different from the one my parents and the church had tried to shape in their image. The conviction grew that I might have some personal power, and though its form and definition were as yet unknown to me, I would trust it. I might have the right to grow and change, and maybe even find a way to articulate what I was discovering as I grew.

INTERVAL

𝕶 *Meditation on a Meditation* 𝕶

For many years I made sporadic attempts to do daily or twice-daily meditation, but all my attempts ended in failure until I found a method that suited me. Failure generally came about by my forgetting to do my meditation, then panicking to make space for it at the far end of the day. This undermined its purpose, which was to steady and deepen me.

The method that worked was one which I found by myself by accident. I started to walk for fifteen or twenty minutes round the block early each morning. This suits me because I'm an early-morning person, and I relish the quiet pre-traffic moments when I can hear the birds, watch the sun rise or see the first light reflected in puddles and observe the rhythmic progress of the seasons. Gradually I started to use my slow walk as a kind of meditation, sometimes simply to quieten the mind and spirit, sometimes to say over to myself words which would ground me in spiritual things and remind me of my true self.

The words that I say have a pattern which varies to a certain degree but stays within the same framework. The first part comes from words I found in the context of psychosynthesis but have since discovered in several other writings on meditation. The last part I've added myself as it came to me.

The words go like this:

> **I have a body, but I am not my body.**
> **I have a mind, but I am not my mind.**
> **I have feelings, but I am not my feelings.**
> **I am spirit.**
> **In this spirit I was born**
> **and grow**

and let go
and die.
In this spirit I am connected with all spirit, alive
and dead.
I am spirit.
I am part of the great spirit.

When I say these things to myself, I know that they're articulating what I feel is the nature of my being. I am, in a sense, enunciating beliefs about myself and the world, though they are not 'beliefs' in the sense of a strict and unchanging creed. The framework of the meditative walk is like the framework of a garden: it has territory and scope, but within that scope I can dig and plant and experiment with change and wait to see what happens and even go back to the original again.

I have a body, but I am not my body. I am telling myself that, though I'm living in my body at present, and most of the time I feel that what happens to my body is happening to *me* (especially when I'm feeling ill, or tense, or when I see a hearse or a grave), an essential element of me – maybe even *the* essential element – is not finally contained in it. I may have existed before I was physically born, and may exist after I die. This doesn't mean that I subscribe wholly to a theory of reincarnation, but it leaves open all the possibilities that lie in that direction.

I give my body a voice, an opportunity to speak to me, to tell me truths about my spirit.

I have a mind, but I am not my mind. I'm a very mind-based person. I tend to judge myself and my worth on the basis of how my mind is functioning. Even in the spiritual sphere, the very writing of this book is a way of giving myself moral and maybe celestial brownie-points for expressing spirituality in a mind-based form. Saying these words reminds me of all the times when I sense life in ways that have nothing to do with the mind: when I laugh, when I love, when I hear the wind in the poplars at the end of the garden, when I stroke the cats, when I apprehend the truth

67

from someone very different from me just by apprehending their spiritual nature.

I ask myself to trust my mind, because it has wisdom over which I have no power of will.

I have feelings, but I am not my feelings. Feelings! These are closest to the spiritual, for me. They seem to be one of the primary vehicles for the spirit. Yet they fling me in all directions, I'm a sailor plunging out towards Fastnet in a Force Ten gale, or I'm locked up in tangled weed in the Sargasso Sea. My feelings are inconstant. When I say these words I remind myself of their inconstancy – at the same time as keeping myself still, quiet, within the feelings as they come: owning them, staying with them, honouring them, saying hello to them and then goodbye – or more usually 'au revoir'.

The discipline of setting up a dialogue with my feelings allows me to let go of some of them for a short time.

I am spirit. This confirms my true identity.

In this spirit I was born. When I come to these words I often find myself smiling. I haven't been through a re-birthing process but I think that, though my early years contained loss and confusion, I was glad to be born. I see dimly that the birth of my soul into this body was a significant and purposeful event, and if it wasn't, I'm going to make it one.

These words mark continuity: the continuity of my soul as I know it now with whatever might come before and after.

In this spirit I grow. This reminds me of growth through the whole of my life. It seems one of the signs of grace that there are so many opportunities for change and growth. There are lots of opportunities for destruction, too. When I say this I'm committing myself to using the opportunities for growth that are offered me, so far as I can, and to turn away from destructiveness. Yet if destruction comes to me maybe that too is part of the process.

In this spirit I let go. It's easiest of all to say these words when I'm walking round the block in the autumn, crunching or squelching the decaying leaves under my feet. I need to be reminded of them often, because I'm a great clinger-on. The up side of that is that I remember things, people, words, events. The down side is that I forget that things and people change, moment by moment. If I am to change and grow, then I have to let go of this moment and pass on to the next one. In the same way I need to let people go, and allow them to let me go. At this point the image of a river sometimes enters in, to loosen me from my moorings, to float or whoosh me forward and on.

In this spirit I die. This is the Big One. As I say this I try to hold it, stay with it, truly know that there will be a time when I am not here, do not exist, am a dead Alison, an ex-Alison. I think of myself in my coffin, and already I'm thinking that I'll hammer on its lid to be let out. I know – I feel – I'm sure – that my spirit will pass through to another existence, but the knowledge flies from me like a lark disappearing up into the distant sky. Occasionally I can hold the knowledge of my death in my awareness for a split second. Then it's gone.

The next best thing is to let myself out through my ears (this is how I feel it happening) and become part of the song of the birds. Then I seem to disappear from the confines of my body-shell and become absorbed into the stuff of the universe.

Sometimes I experiment with saying these phrases the other way round:

**In this spirit I die
and let go
and grow
and am born**.

That's confusing at first, but if I concentrate on each phrase as it comes, it develops its own internal logic.

In this spirit I am connected with all spirit, alive and dead. Now I'm nearing the end of my walk. Often the traffic is building up and I feel myself connected with the people on the bus, with the young man in dark glasses who cycles frantically down the road on his way to the station, with the cycling postman and the paper-boy with his head-phones on. Sometimes I think about what I'm planning to do that day and connect with the people I'm going to meet. I open myself to connection with the huge copper beech tree in the garden on the corner and with the little white terrier that sits on the window-sill of one of the town houses on the last lap of my walk. Sometimes I emphasise my connectedness by saying, 'I am the magpie. I am the rain. I am the montbretia and the petunia. I am the bus and its driver. I am the drain cover.'

I am spirit. I am part of the great spirit. I suppose this is the nearest thing to my 'creed'. If you asked me what it meant, in logical terms, I'd find it difficult to answer. It could imply a 'belief in God'; it certainly is an affirmation of the existence and significance of my soul and of 'Soul'. It's the sum of all the words that come before it; it's the reminder of all the reminders I've given myself about being, living, growing and connecting. If I've got several more minutes to walk I say it to myself over and over again: 'I am spirit. I am part of the great spirit.' Then: 'I am something. I am everything. I am nothing.' Again I nudge against that ultimate, that void where words are paradox, conundrums, koans[1]; that place where there are no words at all.

One morning I walked round my sacred block in the other direction: turned into the main road first, busy even at 7.15, instead of down our quiet side road, and then round the corner by the cypresses and under the deciduous trees, which were busy deciduating because autumn was beginning. And just by that simple expedient – turning everything round by approaching it from the opposite direction – I saw a hundred different things. I walked behind the postman instead of meeting him. I saw the morning light through the thin fading leaves of the ash tree, a small clump of miniature

70

white cyclamen beside a gate-post, reflections of a cherry tree in that always-standing puddle instead of the wall on the other side of it. I missed the bracket fungus on the hawthorn trunk but gained the perfect shape of the sycamore as I approached the corner from along the road. The sun shone through *these* leaves and behind *those* leaves instead of the other way round; it shone through the crawling body of a snail half way across the pavement. Even the stereo effect of traffic and bird-song was the other way round.

When I get home I eat breakfast with Frank, open the post and read the paper, then do a few chores and get down to work and forget my meditation. During the day it often seems as though I haven't said those words or been reminded of the state of my soul. But if I've missed my early morning walk for any reason, I feel as my body feels if it has missed its exercise: stiff, unwieldy. Sometimes, if I'm upset or excited, I simply walk slowly round the block and say nothing at all inside my head. This seems OK too.

5

※

DRAWING A PROFILE FOR THAT
WHICH HAS NO FORM

My younger self fled not toward, but from. . . .
Now I am yearning home, driven as a pigeon
that must align its stubby body with the magnetic
field that feels just right.
(MARGE PIERCY, *'Down the road, down the road'*[1])

This seems the moment, roughly half-way through the story, to
return to language: to assess where I stood in relation to the
religious language I'd been given, and what I was searching for in
a fresh language for my spiritual path.

To write an account like this of a personal spiritual search brings
all sorts of crises of confidence in its train. Not least is the suspicion
that I'm laying a blanket of sweet reasonableness over the messy
bed-linen of actual events; that I'm imposing a cause-and-effect
sequence, ruthlessly if unwittingly erasing all the unrelated or
contradictory pieces of the story. Then there's the arrogance of
the exercise. What is it that's especially deep, especially painful and
exalted about this journey of mine that makes me offer it as
prototype or touchstone for another? Of course I've pre-empted
criticism by expressing the hope that readers will use my account
as a springboard, not a model. How could it be a model? Each life
is so individual. But to 'accept the challenge of self-knowledge', as
Brian Thorne puts it in his Foreword, is also to accept the risk of
failure to know myself: the risk of sliding into ready explanations,
of leaping towards ephemeral goals as though they were eternal
or sentimentalities as though they were truths. The journey is on-
going. What I said in the introductory chapter about the writing
of the book being a process that will bring me to unrecognisable
places is even truer now than when I wrote it.

What were the elements in traditional Christian language that

72

I'd fled from? From hierarchies and creeds, certainly. I didn't want to be servant to a Lord or think of anyone as the Reverend or His Grace. I couldn't articulate what I believed in formal terms. I no longer knelt down beside my bed at night to pray for myself or my friends, though I did hold them lovingly in my thoughts and breathe my own spiritual longings in the depth of the night. I didn't want to be talked at or down to or over the head of: I wanted my own heart to be able to speak and to listen. I knew I was not a 'miserable sinner' as the Anglican prayers made me declare. Though I carried a sense of shame at my shortcomings and mistakes, the shame rose from a sense of contrasting self-worth, of my own essence as a created and creative being, which grew daily with a concept of my life as a journey of discovery. Even in the pit of shame and fear I had some perception that being flung into the pit was part of the journey, part of being whole.

I was in a limbo where communal worship was concerned. When I moved to Yorkshire I didn't rush straight to the nearest religious establishment as I'd done in the past. Sometimes I even stayed in bed on Sunday mornings, which made me remember a friend's remark from student days: 'Does Sunday *have* a morning?' I did attend the parish church sporadically, mainly to find out what social life might be going on around it, but I set off sluggishly compared to my enthusiastic forays into Car Maintenance and Sculpture classes and amateur dramatics. The main goal of my leisure time was to find an attractive and intelligent man to spend my future with. I didn't expect whatever remained of a God 'out there' to help me in finding him.

The new job I'd chosen was possible and even satisfying to do. I was working with the parents of disturbed children attending the Child Guidance service. My intuition had been right. Here was a set-up in which power, though still unequal, seemed to be shared. Families asked for help, they didn't have 'the Council' forced upon them; they made appointments instead of having their emergencies responded to in panic. I and the other members of the team could give time to finding a solution that emerged from the people involved instead of imposing it from outside. On a significant occasion I told one mother that I'd no idea why her seven-year-old son soiled his knickers, I couldn't find anything disturbed in their family history, and I suggested that we while away the hour he spent seeing the psychologist by chatting about this and that. Our conversation turned to recipes. 'Rhubarb crumble? Apple pie?' 'None of mine can stand fruit. Nor vegetables for that matter. What they like is stodge.' It turned out that her son was hopelessly constipated. He wasn't trying to tell his parents something Freudian after all.

I renewed a friendship with a man who had no interest in religion or the church, and though he wasn't right for me in other ways, far too nice and accommodating – I was aware by now of my tendency to be bossy and knew I needed someone who'd stand up to me – I found it refreshing when I was with him not to be wrestling with the meaning of life all the time. And yet . . . I did want to wrestle with it. How could I do that if I couldn't use the language of prayer, either on my own or in church?

Silence

After about six months in the job, and in my spare time acting in plays like *East Lynne* and *An Inspector Calls* in the church hall, I went to morning service one Mothering Sunday. The vicar came straight out of an Alan Bennett satirical sketch, and he was preaching on the glories of motherhood as prototype for the all-powerful, all-caring God. I was not a mother, and I'd long ago reached the point where I felt no trust in my mother or in an intervening, caring God. As the man's voice rose and fell, rose higher and fell lower, I glued myself to the pew with the sweat of anger and vowed never to go back again.

The following weekend my sister was staying with me. I complained about the Alan Bennett vicar. 'What, Ali, have you never been to a Quaker meeting?' she asked. Indeed I hadn't. I spouted my bit about thinking I was not good enough and didn't you have to be born a Quaker? She bundled me into her Morris Minor and drove me to the neighbouring suburb where a one-storey building in somebody's garden served as the Quaker Meeting House. Much later I wrote: 'I'd absolutely no idea what to expect. I knew they sat in silence – but how, without getting bored and without their tummies rumbling? Would someone suddenly leap up and speak in tongues? How would we know when it was all over? We went in and sat down. I sat frozen for ten minutes, waiting for tummy-rumbling and tongue-speaking. Then I began to relax and take it as it came. Nice, ordinary feelings bubbled up. What a relief: no parson telling me what to believe; no worries about the nature of God (He? She?) or Jesus (God? Man?). We just sat, thirty or so of us, in a plain room on a circle of chairs, round a table with a vase of flowers on it. Everyone seemed to be letting the dross of their life settle down so that any gold might begin to show through. After about fifty minutes, some children came in from another room and there were whispers as they showed their parents their paintings. Ten minutes after that, everyone shook hands. Had anyone spoken during the hour? One or two, I think, for a few minutes each. I came away feeling that I'd been at home.'[2]

This, then, was silence. The ultimate act of trust: the absolute surrender of belief, the surrender even of the certainty of words.

Simultaneously I found the silence difficult and knew it was for me. It must have been the incipient feminist in me who was determined to 'minister' – rise to my feet and speak during the hour of worship – in my fourth or fifth meeting, but having got that out of the way I began to free-wheel. I had no scheme for how to use the quiet hour. I thought, I felt, I worried, I meandered, I let go, I hung on. I listened to the two or three or four spoken contributions in each meeting and found that most of them were expressed in the language of daily experience, sometimes supported by a quotation from the Bible or another religious book. I wondered what other people were doing with their silence but, while I appreciated their warm and committed presence round me, I was sure that the responsibility for my hour was my own. I was accountable to no one. I *enjoyed* it. I'd always enjoyed travelling, and this seemed a kind of inward travelling, to an inner landscape which could surprise and scare and bore and thrill me just as an outer landscape could do.

I joined a group of young Quakers and went each week to the volunteer social help outfit that many of them were members of. What attracted me more than anything was how well-informed they were politically, philosophically. Some of them had done a year's overseas aid. They wanted to ask questions about why the British Empire had come and gone or whether it was just conscience-salving to give money to Oxfam. They gardened and wallpapered for old and disabled people without offering prayer in the front room. A lot of them had come to Quakers recently, so that disposed of 'must be born one'; and I found that Quaker toilets used soft toilet paper – quite an event in the '60s – so that got rid of fears that they were impossibly puritanical and good. One of them couldn't take the silence of the Quaker meeting and just came along to the social gatherings and the good works because these people were his friends, and nobody minded.

It was clear that this was what I'd been looking for. Greetings card: *Front* – 'You are the answer to prayer!' *Inside* – 'You're not what I prayed for, but you certainly seem to be the answer.'

Several of the young men there were attractive and intelligent, and one of them seemed emotionally resilient and interested in me. This flip judgement, made during a barn dance in a shambling condemned house in the centre of Leeds which the volunteer group used as their temporary base, has stood me in good stead ever since. It took an astonishingly short time to get to know each other, get engaged and then married. My parents seemed puzzled but accepted it. It was only when they queried the validity of the Quaker marriage ceremony that I realised what a chasm I'd almost casually leapt over, and I wondered at the courage of the Baha'i couple in Edinburgh whose leap had been over some kind of Grand Canyon. After the wedding we moved to Staffordshire, where I applied for membership of the Religious Society of Friends (Quakers) and was accepted.

Revelations

It was when I was doing psychiatric social work in Staffordshire after my marriage that I had a conversion experience – a genuine one, but in a quite different context from the one where I'd spent so many years begging God for the conversion of the dictionary's definition.

I'd found a job in a large Victorian psychiatric hospital and was sent by one of the more sympathetic psychiatrists to chase up an out-patient. I remember that this consultant suffered from Parkinson's disease, and it may have been this that prevented him hiding behind the barrier of arrogance as most of his colleagues did. Before I set off he described this patient to me as a woman in Wolverhampton who'd left her husband, gone to live with her widowed father and been very depressed. The psychiatrist was concerned that she might be suicidal.

I set out, imagining a grim filthy terrace with nappy-buckets overflowing in the hall and a chain-smoking woman soaked in anti-depressants to stave off her despair. I had difficulty finding the house; I was late, and aware that a friend was coming to see us at home that evening and I didn't want to spend too long on this visit. How short a time could I get away with?

It was a terraced house, neat, with an old-fashioned pride about it. A pleasant, quiet-spoken woman greeted me and told me that she'd asked a friend to look after her children so that we could have some peace for talking. Her father was glad to have them living there; he'd been lonely in the years since her mother died, and they could share the responsibilities of the house. She told me about her husband, who had been oppressive though not violent, and how through her religious search – she'd recently joined the Mormons – she'd begun to see herself as too valuable to be put down by him and finally found the courage to make the break.

I was there for about three hours. I just listened while she told me the fairly simple story of her life's discoveries. It got darker and gloomier among her father's big old-fashioned furniture in the front room, but I didn't want to interrupt the flow by suggesting we turn the light on.

By the time I left, I knew all sorts of things that I hadn't known before. I knew that this woman was worthy of complete respect. That she wasn't a 'patient' and I the 'professional', but we were two human beings who could help each other merely by being there when necessary. That people usually don't need advice or cure, but understanding. That this woman's soul was eternal and valuable, and that the hierarchy of social and medical relationships was demeaning to her. That she was my equal, my fellow-soul, and that my soul was also demeaned by my designation as the person who would advise and cure her. That people had their own ways of healing and being healed, which could be released by genuine loving contact with another person. That this contact had probably done more for me than it had done for her, and it was ridiculous that I should be paid for visiting. And so on.

Writing this, I see that a reader's reaction could be, 'Oh, this middle-class social worker was just relieved to find a clean middle-class woman to be visiting rather than a dirty drugged misery.' But I've had other encounters – for instance, with the young mother at the top of the stone stair in St James's in Edinburgh – where

I've felt respect for people living in squalor in much the same way as I felt for the Mormon woman in Wolverhampton. This is the problem with describing seminal experiences: there's a vested interest in defining them as 'one-offs', with the *before* marked off by a sharp line from the *after*. But it's not like that. In the before there are hints and foretastes of the after, and in the after there are echoes of and throw-backs to the before.

I got back very late from Wolverhampton, and fortunately the friend who came to see us at home in Stafford was someone I could describe my feelings to. I don't know whether the woman, whose name and address I've long ago forgotten, had any idea of what she did for me that day, simply by being a whole person and sharing her experiences with me. It certainly was a conversion in the sense that it turned around my view of myself and how I related to the world. I knew that I would eventually give up social work because it involved unequal relationships, and I wanted equal, respectful relationships. This is not to say that all social work is oppressive and patronising. Some people can do it respectfully. What I knew was that I'd been doing it disrespectfully, to boost my own need to feel good, and I couldn't do it any longer.

I knew too that this secular conversion experience had spiritual significance. It was a stage in my progress in learning to love. I couldn't find those sort of words for it at the time, but the experience went into the great pot at the back of my mind, the psycho-spiritual stew from which I hoped eventually to make sense of my soul's travelling.

Before a couple of years were out I was pregnant with our first child and we moved north to the home in which we still live. There, helping Frank to hack off damp plaster and dig up nettles as my increasing bulge would let me, I allowed myself to relish the knowledge that another human being was waiting in my belly.

Having felt no emotional connection until now with the pure, scarcely human figure of Mary, mother of Jesus, there was nothing in the Christian life to convey my exalted sense of being a channel for the emergence of another human spirit. Anglican Christianity – if you ignore the degrading 'churching' of women to cleanse them after childbirth, which has now been replaced, thank goodness, by 'Thanksgiving for the Birth of a Child' – offered no linguistic or ritual means to carry a woman through the transition of child-bearing, still less to carry two parents over into the

unknown area of responsibility for a new life. The religious language I'd inherited dealt in certainties, in arrivals; not in journeys,
transitions.

Only years later did I find poems to express it. Like Joan
Benner's 'Girl with a 'cello':

> Some personal, insistent Gabriel
> compels the daily weaving of a habitation
> for air, brings with him the enigma and the weight
> of a growing conception.
> And she is vulnerable because, scarcely become,
> she is taken over by another. . . .
> Yet, as her hands mould and set the string in motion,
> she draws a profile for that which has no form:
> air moves at her shaping
> from breath to word.[3]

And after our daughter was born:

> you fell asleep drinking
> from my breast, drinking
> nourishment & warmth & a
> new mothers growing love.
> it was not stained glass
> windows: it was the pressure
> & release of milk from
> my body to yours: our
> deep communion.[4]

A revelation came within seconds of her birth. I could say it
came together with, at the moment of, her birth. It came in the
form of the strongest possible feeling – undeniable – that this
fresh-born human being was not new, that she had come from
somewhere, that she was totally herself despite, not because of or
as well as, her genetic inheritance from her father and me.

I have heard of other instances: a new-born baby who gave
her mother a look of such complete wisdom that it was almost
frightening. When people ask me if I believe in life after death I
answer, 'I have no knowledge of it. I do have knowledge of life
before birth, which opens the doors to anything.'

The importance of this experience lay not in the 'belief' aspect
but in the way it changed me. I'd always longed for children of

my own, feeling that bearing them and bringing them up would make my rather doubtful life unquestionably worthwhile. But now I knew that this child was not in any sense 'mine'. I shouldn't, couldn't mould her into my way of being, because she had her own being which I must respect. She would develop her own ways of expressing that being. My job was to care for her during the time she needed it; to keep my channel as clean as possible so as to allow her wisdom to flow through.

These perceptions were all confirmed when our second, very different daughter was born.

Two years later, my mother died after much illness, and two years after that my father was found in his kitchen dead from a rupture of the heart. Perhaps because so many events followed on so rapidly from each other, this was a time of revelations.

My mother's death couldn't be unexpected because she'd been ill for so long, but the impact of it was enormous. We didn't reach the hospital – in Barrow-in-Furness, an hour and a quarter's drive from their Lake District home – in time for the moment of her death, but the hospital staff asked us if we would like to see her. My father spent some time with her; my sister, being a nurse, knew what death looked like and said she'd rather not. I felt I needed to see her. Standing beside her tiny empty body, I felt 'knowledge' again. I knew that Mother was not in that body, and that I would die one day too.

This knowledge of death has stayed in me less securely than my knowledge of birth, of my children's separate identity, because my body and my brain rebel against the awareness of mortality. But I knew it, and again the knowledge changed me. I knew as Nekhlyudov did in Tolstoy's *Resurrection*: 'He recognised the familiar features and could scarcely believe his own eyes. Yesterday he had seen this face angry, excited, full of suffering. Now it was quiet, motionless and terribly beautiful. . . . "Why had he suffered? Why had he lived? Does he understand now what it's all for?" thought Nekhlyudov, and it seemed to him that there was no answer, that there was nothing but death, and he felt faint.'[5] And it changed me like it changed the woman in Jackie Kohnstamm's story of a very different mother-daughter relationship: 'I realise with a shock that you have left me here, alone. . . . But with that thought comes another one, terrifying in its clarity: in time I shall learn to live a new life, a full one, unrestricted by your fears, and this I shall only be able to do because you are no longer here.'[6] There was the sense of relief, of being released.

The second death, of my father, suddenly, was doubly shocking. My Quaker Meeting lovingly supported me, and so did other Quakers I'd got to know around the country. At my father's funeral, with the village church packed to the thick stone walls and the congregation following the coffin up the steep slippery churchyard in the winter weather to the rectangle of deeply-dug earth at the top – the grave dug by old Tom who had nodded silent greetings to him Sunday by Sunday in the church porch, the coffin carried by the joiner and the plasterer he'd known for years – I realised that 'the parish', which I'd experienced as a patriarchal and often oppressive entity, could be a genuine community of the spirit. The vicar who had been my father's close friend and fell-walking companion was no longer the incumbent, but I remembered him as a proper pastor, a loving shepherd to his flock; and the flock were a busy, quarrelsome, thriving body of people joined by proximity and a commitment to the landscape of their birth or adoption as well as to the God of their forefathers. It was a wholly different spiritual community from the community of choice that I'd found at the Quaker Meeting. It was not for me, for all sorts of personal and historical reasons, but here I was seeing it united in shock and grief.

'You're an orphan now,' said my children, and it brought home to me that, at thirty-two, I was now of the uppermost generation in my family. Again, the acquisition of responsibility seemed a spiritual transition for which no traditional words or ritual were available. There were times when, despite all the love, I felt very alone. I had settled in as a Quaker, and the awareness bore in on me that my spiritual journey was my own. I had a right to it, and it had a right to take me forward into whatever known or unknown paths it willed. There is something extraordinarily lonely about that realisation. The philosopher Heidegger uses the word *Geworfenheit* – 'thrown-ness' – to express the feeling that we are hurled into the world, without a by-your-leave, quite alone. At this point I felt not only hurled into, but hurled around in the world. I knew that some of my Quaker friends felt 'led' into specific paths, but I'd never experienced that and would have felt suspicious of it if I did. I almost chose to be hurled.

Reclaiming my journey, recognising the Other

I wrote *it* just now: 'my spiritual journey was my own. I had a right to it, and it had a right to take me forward into whatever known or unknown paths it willed'. By 'it', do I mean 'God'? I think I mean 'life'. Life moved me on. Maybe by the leadings that I'd heard about but couldn't accept, maybe by unconscious intention, or maybe by chance, I was moved on.

Perhaps I'm offered a job. Or I find I am pregnant. Perhaps two people I know have quarrelled irreconcilably; a friend suddenly needs me; the phone rings and I learn that someone close to me is dying. When these things happen I can't respond habitually: I'm pushed forward into new responses, my spirit is taxed in new ways. These are the outer elements.

Then there are the inner ones. The rhythm of growth and ageing, certainly, but also the rhythms of the spirit by which I know, or feel, or hope or fear, that I must change. I must move into a different way of being, or be still and absorb the importance of where I stand now.

The gradual realisation that this was all up to me, that I could no longer blame a hierarchical religious establishment for not allowing me to develop spiritually, was a challenge as well as a relief. It felt like an exercise in reclamation. But there was a reciprocal side. If I was responsible for my soul, if no one could deny my experience or the language I might find to express it in, then so was everyone else responsible for their souls, and I had no right to deny their experience or language either.

Here the challenge took on gargantuan dimensions. It was the challenge of George Eliot's 'equivalent sense of self' which falls 'with a certain difference'.[7] In reading *Middlemarch* I can easily empathise with the lively, intensely feeling character of Dorothea. I can readily acknowledge her sense of self. But how can I at the same time, and equivalently, acknowledge the different sense of self of her dry, cold, old husband Casaubon?

That's the challenge of the unattractive. There is also the challenge of the unfamiliar, which I'm tempted to dismiss as simply wrong. Then there's the challenge of echoes of the past, which I've found can provoke unnervingly powerful reactions.

Because of my 'refugee' status in the community of Friends, I was apt to rail against any spoken ministry that smacked of the parsonical. Quotations from the Bible, even prayer, I could tolerate if they were offered as a personal insight. But if anyone so much as implied that I and the others present must agree with whatever was being said I would sit there, seething with resentment, using my precious hour of quiet to work out the exact wording by which I would demand a retraction as we drank our coffee afterwards. I knew that demands for retraction were out of order in this tolerant atmosphere, and over coffee I generally tended to get talking to someone more congenial. But there came a time when two of the more regular 'ministers' drove me to distraction. Literally, they distracted me from the proper business of the Quaker meeting for worship. They were both men. One of them seemed approachable, and I approached him. I was angry and he was hurt. We parted with me feeling a certain sense of satisfaction. A few days later I got a letter from him telling me that he still felt hurt, and doubted if he could ever minister again. The heavens fell in on me. I was desperately ashamed. He suggested that we meet, and we did, and had a real exchange of views and experiences many of which had little to do with the matter in question. I began to understand where he was coming from, and he understood me in return. After some remaining uneasiness we were able to talk more easily and openly.

The second one was more problematic because the man concerned didn't take part in the social life of the Meeting. I decided I would refer the matter to the elders, whose job is to care for the spiritual life of the Meeting. I'd put a stop to this, I thought. He was upsetting a lot of other people besides me. Yes, he'd probably be hurt – but too bad, he should be made to realise the harmful effect he was having. I resolved to act soon, knowing that I was right.

I was getting dressed one morning when the revelation came. It came to me from some deep inner source that this man had as much right to express his spiritual insights in his own words as I had. I knew how I would feel if I was told to be silent because what my spirit said – or, if you like, what the Spirit said through me – was judged unacceptable to the ears of others. That judgement had been delivered to me for years in the very structure of the churches where I'd struggled to be a faithful member. Was I now going to say it to someone else? My favourite motto in the peace movement was 'You can't kill the spirit'. But you can try. It had been tried on me. Was I now going to try to kill, too?

After that revelation, I couldn't do it. I could have said to the man, 'Your words are not for me at the moment. Please don't include me in them'. I didn't: my courage failed me. But I knew that I must accept his words as a genuine expression of his individual spiritual experience, not grudgingly but with real respect. If I couldn't offer him that sort of respect there was no reason why he should offer it to me. Then I would be lost, because respect was what I'd been looking for on this long journey. I wasn't going to give it up just at the point when I had found it at last.

Respect is at the heart of my search. The respect of other people is what allows me to reclaim my own spirituality. I am 'allowed', not in the sense of being offered tolerant or patronising permission, but of being freed, of being set free. Within the Quaker Meeting, in my work and within my married partnership I've been given this freedom. Because it's a gift of such incalculable value I want to give it to other people. It involves the setting aside of judgement – something I've always found difficult – and the slow and painful acquisition of a real acceptance of difference.

It is also the freedom to step over the edge of words: to hang on when the words break down, to allow myself to ask questions where there may not be an answer, to wait in the aching void. At the time of my parents' deaths, and times before and since then when realities have surged into me on their own momentum – the realities of death and abandonment and aloneness in the midst of difference and strangeness – I have felt, in abandoning the role of a child of God, like an orphan of the Spirit.

Yet I have come up against a wordless, soundless, lightless wave which envelops me even while I carry on an outwardly active life. At the opposite end of the spectrum but not so very different in quality, there has been intense light, vivid sound, waves of exalted feeling that again could find no articulation. And there are the confusions, the paradoxes, the tension of experiences that are so suffusing and non-linear that the prospect of putting one mark after another on the page to express them, or sounds from the vocal chords in some sort of order, is simply unthinkable. Then I must wait, and maybe – or maybe not – discover some sort of trust in the waiting.

6

FIRST AND LAST MYSTERIES

It is my love I hold back
hide
not wanting to be seen
scrawl of hand
writing
don't guess
don't guess at my
passion
a wholly wild and raging
love for this world.

(SUSAN GRIFFIN, '*Prayer for Continuation*'[1])

So far the story has been roughly chronological. I've been looking at key experiences in my first thirty or more years and making some sense of where they took me in spiritual terms: that is, finding terms in which to express them spiritually, and perhaps even coming to terms with them personally. I now have to look at more problematic aspects, where chronology isn't appropriate because the threads in the fabric of time have got muddled. If the chronological method doesn't work here, I'll need to take themes and find autobiographical illustration, rather than describing events and then drawing themes out of them.

It has dawned on me as I've been writing that, in looking at spiritual and religious language, I've sidestepped the two areas that many people associate most closely with religion: theology, and ecstatic experience.

To take theology first. My dictionary gives these definitions of theology: '1. the systematic study of the existence and nature of the divine and its relationship to and influence upon other beings. 2. the systematic study of Christian revelation concerning

God's nature and purpose, esp. through the teaching of the Church.'[2]

I've always found the first-definition kind of theology difficult to handle, because it's an ' -ology' of something that we can't prove, and because we can't be sure when we talk about the divine that we each mean the same thing. The second definition is easier. The study of what people have *said* about the Christian God is handleable in a way that simply 'God' or 'the divine' is not.

What I miss in traditional theology is the verb arising from the noun. My dictionary gives the verb 'to theologise', but I've never heard it used. One of the few sayings about God that I can accept without question is 'God is a verb, not a noun'. Theology uses words that baffle me, like hermeneutics and soteriology and theodicy; it draws distinctions that I can never remember, like between deism and theism. I realise that my difficulties may come from the fact that I'm intellectually not up to it, and I apologise to theologians like Daphne Hampson, whose *Theology and Feminism*[3] I did enjoy. But in the end when I grapple with theology I seem to be grappling with a fog.

Philosophy, in contrast, appeals to me, despite some equally baffling terminology. Most of it seems to be about real questions – in fact it can easily subsume theology under its capacious wing – and it comes ready furnished with the verb 'to philosophise'. I appreciate philosophy. Philosophising strikes me as a vigorous, rigorous activity in which there needn't be winners and losers. I like the moral philosophers because they ask the questions I find most interesting. I like the existentialists particularly because they're so challenging, so uncompromising: they refuse to let us slide into dishonesty or self-deception, into what they call 'bad faith'. Because I've inherited my mother's ability to put things into tidy forms of words, the besetting temptation for me is to think that the word is all, that once something has been encapsulated in phrases then nothing more needs to be felt or explored. Existentialist philosophy challenges me to confront the sentimentality of this way of being, to recognise paradox and the necessity for change. Above all it drives me to face the fact that much of my life is not forced upon me but is of my own choosing.

If I am drawn to vigorous, rigorous questioning, then I'm forced up against Jennifer's challenge in Chapter 4. She described herself as 'non-religious'. I decline to call myself 'religious' because that brings with it an expectation of absolute belief, a kind of party loyalty. So I use the word 'spiritual': I say that I'm 'on a spiritual journey', to indicate that I am 'open to new [spiritual] light, from whatever source it may come'.[4] But what is it that separates me from the morally and socially responsible person who declines to use a concept of spirituality, who can't think of their existence in terms of a soul at all, who sees the aspects of humanity that I lump together under the heading 'soul/spirit' as coming from the astonishing interaction of millions of synapses in the human nervous system and a wonderfully evolved biochemistry? If I'm honest, the only answer to this is that *I choose to be so separated*.

I choose to make a difference in assumption. When I reflect on the scope of my life, I assume a before-and-after. I have no proof of this one way or the other, though I've met people who have described experiences of contact with people beyond this life. I have never had these specific experiences, but I do live as if there was a time – as if there were experiences – before birth, and that there will be times and experiences after death. I'm fairly sure that those who describe themselves as non-spiritual would part company with me at this point. Maybe some who describe them-selves as spiritual would part company too. There are no fixed cut-off points.

I also find myself living as if there are means of communication other than the physical. Again, I've had no specific telepathic or out-of-the-body experiences. But I assume that if I hate someone it will harm them, and if I love someone they will benefit even when I'm out of their company. I assume that, just as the flutter of a butterfly's wings in China may reverberate to cause a whirl-wind in the Atlantic, so every thought and feeling of mine goes into the great maelstrom of Spirit and has its effect.

I've used the words 'assume' and 'assumption' here. Don't I mean 'believe' and 'belief'? I don't think so. There is nothing fixed about it. Growth and change are for me the keys, and though I'd be loath to give up my assumptions (maybe because they're such a comfort, as the sceptics would point out) I would be prepared to change them if events or inner promptings moved me to change them.

There's another strand to the journey that an observant reader may have noticed, and it's one which can bring me together again with my morally responsible non-spiritual friend and with my friends within the Christian and other faiths. I could describe it as a rule of thumb, and it goes like this: if my assumption, provable or not, is likely to lead to my becoming a more loving person, then it's a pretty good one to base my attitudes and behaviour on, though it still needs monitoring to make sure that I'm not kidding myself in any way. For instance, my 'knowledge' that my children came from somewhere, that they have independent souls which I do not own and cannot control: this may help me not to be possessive and authoritarian in my ways of bringing them up. Similarly, if I respect other people because they have a spark of the divine within them, it helps me to listen to them or care for them and prevents me fighting wars against them.

I'm sure the philosophers will tell me there are a thousand problems of definition in that rule of thumb, that this way has been trodden many times before and been found to have potholes and pitfalls galore. But if I'm being honest about a language for my personal journey through life, and if I'm grappling with the intellectual side of it, that's where I'm standing at the moment.

Ecstatic religious experience

When I read about the peak experiences which people like William James have designated religious, I find myself with a strong sense of envy. Despite my awareness of waiting in the void, waiting in the light, I've had no absolute, definitive moments of this sort. 'It was as though my spirit was translated completely out of my body into a world of entirely new dimensions, a world in which time, as we know it, had no significance and in which for the first time in my life I felt completely and vitally conscious of everything which was going on about me. I seemed to be pulsing with a new and hitherto unexperienced vitality and to feel completely effective and master not only of my own destiny but of the entire destiny of the universe. Yet I, as an individual ego, no longer had any substance; I was part of the process of creation which was a combination of love and strength and humility; something infinitely gentle, infinitely wise and infinitely and eternally at peace with itself. . . . There was no longer any good or evil – the riddle of both seemed to be solved. There was no longer any light or darkness . . . no birth or death, beginning or end. . . . That moment was eternity.'[5]

Not having known a moment like that, I wonder whether this journey of mine through questions of language and meaning might be superfluous if I had. It might be like the conversion that my evangelical friends insisted on, but it would come from inside myself, not outside, and so it would carry more conviction because no Outside Being was in control to change or redefine it. I'm aware that I may be idealising, perhaps romanticising. I long to *know*, just as these people are able to know, absolutely, incontrovertibly, in a way that no subsequent experience can overthrow. I've written about 'knowing', yes; but my knowledge has not been instantaneous or absolute. I can be cast into self-doubt by the force of argument or by contradictory experience. My children seem to have no memory or knowledge of lives before this one. Neither do I. So where does that leave the knowledge that came with their birth? Yet it happened. I knew then, and I don't deny the knowledge now. Similarly Jane Sherwood, who wrote vividly about communicating by 'automatic writing' with T. E. Lawrence after his death,[6] said to friends many decades later that she looked back on the episode with surprise, but could only accept simply that it had happened.

I come back again and again to the fact that I am not a philosopher or a theologian, or even a researcher into religious experience, but a spiritually minded individual in search of an honest language. I'm also a writer of fiction and drama, and that provides me with a metaphor for the search. The process of writing is, to me, a wonderful and mysterious business, and depends not on theory or analysis but on the realisation – the making real – of character and story. It's a process which relates language to life creatively. So it feels closely linked to the way in which my reliance on religious belief has changed into a trust in experience and growth.

Writing: the mystery of creativity

When I write a story or a play, the first thing to come out on to paper is generally a cliché or a stereotype. 'This is a new character, a new story, a new idea about what is interesting or exciting or moving or funny,' I say to myself. 'How shall I express it? Oh!' I think, panicking at all this newness, 'so-and-so said something slightly similar, and she expressed it like this. . . .' And I write down something very like that. I write in the style of Fay Weldon or Alan Bennett or Toni Morrison. Or I write sub-sub Fay/Alan/Toni; often sub-*Neighbours*. Then an inner voice says, 'No, it's not quite like that. . . .' I panic again. I don't know what to write. But I'm experienced enough now to be able to leave it to soak in the sludge at the bottom of my mind. If I've got a deadline to meet, I say to my mind as I go to sleep, 'Come on, Mind, see if you can come up with a clue to this character/plot/theme by tomorrow morning'. And, miraculously, the mind does. Maybe not tomorrow morning, but often soonish, though occasionally (if I don't have a deadline) not for twenty years.

What seems to be happening is that the accretion of other writers' works, the words that I've absorbed over years of reading and listening and watching, have enlightened me. They've said to me, 'This is how things are around this neck of the woods. This is how it might be for you.' They've tapped the mystery and passed it through the channels of their souls, and in doing so they've passed on some of the mystery to me. The mystery first strikes me in a moment of brilliant insight or deep movement of feeling; then it hardens into a Belief that, if that is how things were for these brilliant people, that is how it must be for me too. But – as my mind eventually tells me, if I listen – the mystery has its own channel to my soul. If I wait, and trust, it can pour itself down in my own words.

That channel is vital. The existence of the channel doesn't guarantee that everything I write is in some way sacred: by no means. But it does mean that some bits of it (and I'm not always sure which bits) are real. Sometimes the reality doesn't shine through until the seventh or the seventy-seventh draft; then my patience and my trust are tested to the limit.

It often seems to me that my job as a writer is not to 'create' as such. It's to keep that channel clean and clear: to keep it in touch with the channels of others but distinct from theirs, a conduit in the great network of conduits. If my channel is clear, then the mystery will flow through it and down it.

I find it revealing to read what other writers say about this mystery. Here is Rose Tremain: 'One rainy afternoon in August 1983, I lay down in a hotel bedroom in Bourges and had a waking dream. . . . It was what I shall call the "first mystery" of the book [*The Swimming Pool Season*], the thing that will – or might – contain the essence of what that book is going to be. . . . For *Sacred Country*, alone among the six novels I've written, there does not seem to be any "first mystery". There is just the complex idea of the unsynchronized life and around that fixed edifice a lot of unruly traffic has to pass and re-pass in opposite directions. But, looking back now at the shape of the novel, I am beginning to wonder whether there isn't something called a "last mystery", which may only become clear after all sound of traffic has ceased.'[7]

There's a misconception that's often repeated about the mystery of writing: that if you are alone, and if you wait, if no one phones and there's someone else to do the cleaning, then you will be inspired and those words will be sacred for ever more. It's not true. It's true that you must scribble things down when inspiration comes, and that you must keep those scribbles because they're vitally important. But the truth of what I'm writing may come in a workshop, at someone else's instigation or provocation, or it might be prompted by an editor or director. The truth of these individual characters and this specific narrative can be the result of intense searching, or discursive exploration, or random experiment. Characters especially have to be discovered, like living people, by friendship, by getting in touch to find out how they are, by asking what they would feel like if a crane-load of melons fell on them or their lifelong companion turned out to have a history as a shoplifter of which they were completely unaware. The truth of a character or an image or a vision may be locked away and inaccessible except by approaching it sideways, by contrast, by shock, by pressing a discipline on it, by confronting it with monsters or banalities, or by sitting patiently waiting for it to come out of its cave.

So it is with my spiritual life. When I try to explain my spiritual experience to myself or other people, the words that come out first are the words that have been given to me by someone else. The experience is new, different, extraordinary: it hasn't a parallel in the world I see around me. I might want to say, 'I saw a tree, and I knew it was that tree, and I wanted to hug it.' What? I can't say *that*. What shall I say? I'll say: 'We ought to feel at one with Nature; in our day and age, the environmental problems are such that we must develop a spiritual awareness of ecology.' I preach a sermon. I offer a prescription. I develop a belief.

It takes all my courage to own my experience, to accept it as real, however strange or difficult it is to explain – even, sometimes, to remember – and to find my own words for it. What are my words, anyway? It's risky to look for them, even riskier to find them. It means I've got to articulate my distinct peculiarities, and these might turn out to be unacceptabilities. If I articulate them I lay myself open to ridicule. I remember the ridicule I experienced as a child – it always astonishes me how readily adults set about ridiculing children's observations and insights – and I'm afraid.

Then comes the next stage: the dismay when the words are available but don't convey my insight, when they look back at me as flat, devoid of inspiration. Worse, they're still the words of other people. Or, if they're different, they sound poeticised, forced, fancy, pretentious.

That's the point where I have to apply the discipline of waiting, or the different discipline of contrast or shock, or by sidling up to it and gently teasing out its deeper meaning.

If I ride the fear, wait patiently in discipline, I will find the words that are my words. They might not find a listener, but it may be enough if I speak them or write them just for me. If I am faithful, what is beyond words will shine through.

My ultimate dream is this: that if I keep the channels clear and dedicate myself to looking for the truth of things and the love in things, then the words will flow true; and that the person I'm with, today or tomorrow, or the person who reads my words in some future time, will recognise what I'm trying to say and be encouraged to find their own words to say what different love and unfamiliar truth they've discovered for themselves. Then all the words can be recognised in an atmosphere of loving acceptance, so that they can be carried from one person to another with all the spirit that no words can convey, and a spiritual community will be formed.

Sex . . .

I've already written about the confusion and connection that I've found, in my thinking and my life, between religion and sex. I'd like to return now to that theme in more depth.

Two incidents, both from my own life:

The first: It's the late 1950s. A sixth-form Chaplain's Discussion Group at a private girls' school. The subject: the Sacrament of Holy Communion. No one is interested. Recent visiting chaplains have been quite intelligent, even sexually attractive. The chaplain today is neither.

'How do you feel, girls, personally,' he asks, 'about that moment of communion – that special moment of contact with God?'

Embarrassment; eyes glazing in fascination at sandalled feet; giggles hidden behind hands.

Sheila speaks. Sheila is 3rd year Sixth, bored; marking time, heading for Oxford. 'I've heard,' she says, 'that if you're truly religious, taking Communion can be really uplifting. Ecstatic, even. A bit like orgasm. Could you comment on that, sir?'

The chaplain blushes to the roots of his hair. Or I presume he does: I'm so confused that I can't see or hear anything more for the rest of the session.

The second: Two women talking. One: 'I've always known that my spirituality is my centre, my core, the one place where they can't touch me, where I'm real, where I'm safe, where I can explore or be still, where I can just *be*.'

The other: 'I've always known that my sexuality is good, is at the centre of my life and being, that it's an energy to be explored and known. But I mustn't tell *them* about it because, if they knew, it would be invaded and derided and denied. I know that it must be celebrated, because it is life.'

The traditional religious view is that life-energy is finite: that if you 'dissipate' your energies on sex, there will be less or none 'left' for the spiritual side of life. This assumption underlies some of the negative urgings towards celibacy (though there are positive ones too) and the more ludicrous notions about masturbation, that it opens a psycho-physiological tap and drains away one's moral fibre.

But if I try flipping this idea on to its reverse side, I open my eyes in wonder. Could it be that sexual and spiritual energy come from the same source, and that that same source is infinite?

My reaction is, 'Oh glory!' Relief. A withering of guilt. A

vision of the additive, the positive, the flowing, in place of the divisive and the negative and the stuck.

Since I was released from the prison of being an inhibited small child trying to win favour by being good, I've realised the passions that lay beneath that inhibited shell. My passions have presented me and those close to me with all sorts of problems. But I've become aware that the different parts of my personality are so interwoven that the passionate part can't be denied without my creative side – in relationships as well as in writing – also being denied. I'm aware of the hurt that my passions can cause. So I listen carefully when I hear a hostile reaction to theories of the unity of sexual and spiritual energy. 'But sex is so dangerous!' It is. The release of sexuality from its inhibitions can lead to emotional anguish, unwanted pregnancy, sexually transmitted diseases, to unbearable strain on relations within a family and community. These are powerful reasons for keeping it under every kind of moral, social, conceptual and linguistic restraint. I have felt that restraint, and known the safety of being good. It was impossible for me to stay there, but I know that it had advantages in terms of not being openly hurt and not openly hurting other people.

But there are consequences, too, of sexual repression and guilt: consequences like rape, exploitative sex, self-disgust, chronic hypocrisy. Religious institutions have been the most powerful instruments of repression and guilt. They have denied a conceptual language that expresses the interplay of sexual and spiritual energies. Instead, religion has used the language of gender-based dominance and submission to enforce codes of behaviour as if they had eternal validity. The norms of other times, other cultures – the free homosexuality of the ancient Greeks, examples of polygamy such as in Islam or the early Mormons (and the much rarer examples of polyandry), the easy sexual experiments among the Samoan adolescents whom Margaret Mead studied, as well as extreme versions of the suppression of female sexuality like infibulation and clitoridectomy – have all been rationalised by the religious codes of their society.

Enough has been written about this, in plays like Mary O'Malley's *Once a Catholic* and fiction such as Brian Moore's, in Nawal el Saadawi's writing, and not least in Anthony Faulkner's moving book in this series, for me not to dwell on it. But I can't resist one example from a favourite poet, John Donne, who wrestled

more openly with his sexual and spiritual divisions than almost
any other. When in the full flow of sexual love he wrote:

> But O alas, so long, so farre,
> Our bodies why doe wee forbeare?
> . . . We owe them thankes, because they thus,
> Did us, to us, at first convay,
> Yeelded their forces, sense, to us. . . .
> Loves mysteries in soules doe grow,
> But yet the body is his booke.[8]

Later, after his religious conversion, it was different:

> Wilt thou forgive that sinn, by which I'have wonne
> Others to sinn, and made my sinn their dore?
> Wilt thou forgive that sinn which I did shunne
> A year or twoe, but wallowed in a score?
> When thou hast done, thou hast not done,
> >   For I have more.[9]

. . . and sexuality

So: if I am liberal and liberated – which clearly I am, or aim to
be – what is the way out of this conundrum? In searching for a
way forward in the language we use, I've taken a long ramble
around what we mean when we use the word *sex*.

'Sex', as a trigger-word, sets off visions of people *doing it*.
Putting bits of themselves into one another and drawing bits of
other people into themselves – having it off, putting it about,
fornicating, committing adultery or acts of gross indecency, giving
officials in courts of law and PhD students of D. H. Lawrence
cause to debate whether penetration actually took place or not.

But sex – sexuality – encompasses infinitely more than acts of
penetration. For me it is the greatest of passions and connected
with every other passion. Sexuality is relationship, connection,
forward-thrusting direction. It is an energy which fires human
motivation from birth until death. It involves wordless communications, subliminal perceptions; it reveals more than the eye can
see or the ear can hear. It is an acutely sensitive bodily and psychic
awareness. It involves frustration and satisfaction and tranquillity
and ecstasy. To deny it is to deny life.

95

As we live, we are transmitters of life.
And when we fail to transmit life, life fails to flow through us.
That is part of the mystery of sex, it is a flow onwards.
Sexless people transmit nothing.[10]

When in 1991 I was researching my play *Heretics*[11] about a gay man who wanted to be ordained and at the same time be open about his gay partnership, I began to understand how many levels existed on which sexuality could be denied. It could be eradicated completely, as if by surgical operation. I couldn't talk to people who had done this because by definition it was a process of total denial. But I recognised the process, and I heard a comment about it that I found enlightening: 'The trouble with so many clergy is that they're *not all there*. How can they exude the love of God if they're only half a person?' Other gay clergy did acknowledge their needs and passions and were even able to be honest about them to some very close friends. But most of their days were spent living out a lie.

It is not only gay clergy who have to repress their sexuality, and it was not only sexuality they had to deny. It was also their basic human warmth. I learnt how unwise it was for clergy to become close enough to any parishioner to be able to call them 'friend'. This was only partly a question of sexual temptation; there was also the danger of allegations of favouritism. So clergy had to deny themselves warmth and closeness at the same time as advocating warmth and closeness for others. It was obvious that the strain on the only permitted intimate relationship, marriage, could become intolerable. Even that relationship wasn't allowed the other great intimacy: the spontaneous energy of irritation and anger.

Not for the first time I had the glimmerings of a vision: that we might become aware of our sexual energies and harness them and celebrate them; that we might know ourselves on a day-to-day basis, and accept ourselves, as sexual as well as spiritual beings; that we needn't question ourselves constantly about which is which, or divide body from soul, but could allow the energy to flow freely and creatively within ourselves and out, in gentleness and openness, towards other people.

To do this, the feeling itself needs to be distinguished from the reaction to that feeling: first to acknowledge and absorb the feeling, and then – only then – ask questions about how to react to the feeling. To feel first, and then ask, on the basis of love and care for all the people involved, what to do, how to act.

Some people's sexuality is in harmony with the expectations of their community. What proportion are they? We have no way of telling. There are no definitive social surveys. We can only discover these things from fiction, drama, poetry and biography. Writers perhaps overstate the tensions and confusions of the sexual life; there aren't many good plots in the celebration of quiet conformist content. But the opposite may also be true: that secret desires, fears and couplings may be more common than we realise. Like the situation John Berger describes in *A Fortunate Man*: 'One day [the doctor] was called to a couple of old-age pensioners. They had lived in the Forest for thirty years. Nobody had anything very special to say about them . . . A long time before, the wife had worked as a maid in the big house of a near-by village. The husband had worked on the railway. The husband said that his wife "was bleeding from down below". – Sassall talked to her a little and then asked her to undress so that he could examine her. He went into the kitchen to wait until she was ready. There the husband looked at him anxiously . . . When he went back into the parlour, the wife was lying on the ottoman. Her stockings were rolled down and her dress up. "She" was a man. He examined her. The trouble was severe piles. Neither he nor the husband nor she referred to the sexual organs which should not have been there.'[12]

A story like this carries me so far from straightforward 'Christian morality' and the sentimentality of 'family values' that I can't find my way back. I have many friends with many different sorts of partnerships and relationships, who experience sexual connection with their own or the opposite sex or with both, with one partner or more. My own feelings are of a greater variety and depth than I would have guessed possible. I cannot judge: I can only try to respect and understand.

. . . and sensuality, and pain

My passionate argument is this: that if we accept the common source of both spiritual and sexual energy, if we acknowledge and accept sexual feelings as valuable, as integral, then we can be fully open to the sensual. Instead of denying the earth and our relationship with it – our animal nature, the soil and its fruits, the rhythm of the seasons and the nutritional cycle, the necessity for waste, decay and destruction as well as growth and fruitfulness – we can welcome them.

We yearn for unity with our origin, the source of ourselves. If we achieve oneness with another human being, the experience can seem the nearest we can go towards that unity. Dervla Murphy expresses this feeling wonderfully clearly in her autobiography: 'I remember my exultant sense of kinship with everything I saw – with the sheep and the crows and the stream by the track and the rocks and the heather and the clouds in the sky. I felt that until this day I had been only half-alive, half-aware; now I had a new relationship not just with Godfrey but with all of nature.'[13] I've felt that 'exultant sense of kinship'. I've felt, too, a sense that in losing myself in sexual desire and in the fulfilment of the sexual act I'm nearer to death than at any other moment in my life so far. It is the death of self-consciousness, of ego; the losing of myself as a drop of water is lost in the river, yet not lost, not vanished or swallowed, but wholly absorbed into a wider, deeper, more rushing and ultimate essence and power.

The physicality or spirituality of a relationship need not be defined or separated; still less need the two – body and spirit – be set in opposition to each other. Celibacy too has great value, if it is a celibacy of choice. The Boston Women's Collective say that 'many of us have found that periods of celibacy, a month, a year, or even longer – can be freeing and growth-producing. We are freed to explore ourselves without the problems and power struggles of a sexual relationship. We can begin to define ourselves not just in terms of another person.'[14]

Sometimes the feelings associated with sexuality are the opposite of exultancy and fulfilment: they are pain, anger, powerlessness and fear. Sex is wielded abusively in our society as an instrument of oppression, working on every level down to the deepest self-hatred. For people who have experienced that humiliation it can seem impossible to stay with the feelings that the memories engender. It is a miracle if the hurt individual can find a safe person to share their memories with, a safe place without an atmosphere of oppressive power, and enough time to go right through the feelings till there comes a level where the outside world can be re-entered without panic. If the feelings are acknowledged, lived through, held in trust, it may be possible to move into a loving relationship.

A task for those of us who work with language and describe our lives as a spiritual journey might be to explore the language of sexual expression and try to find words that are not oppressive but respectful, mutual and loving.

With passionate sexual love there is always the risk of loss, through a change in the nature of the relationship, through parting, or through death. The novelist Ann Oakley has explored the pain and contradictions and tentative resolution of the ending of love in a way that speaks to me: 'She had reclaimed and not lost a part of herself, while remaining grateful to him for the way he had loved her, without which she would never have stood and faced herself. – "Remember me", she would have said to him, had she given herself or him the chance. . . . "What has been should not be regretted. The proper use of memory is for liberation – from false hopes of the future as well as from enslavement to past actions and desires. Did we love or only desire? Don't let your memory rewrite the past. Remember me".'[15] *She had reclaimed and not lost a part of herself.*

The language that religion has used towards things sexual has been the language of judgement, not of understanding. My sister wrote to the Archbishop of Canterbury at a time when the Church of England reaffirmed its ruling on the permanence of marriage vows and denied divorced people the right to remarry in church. She wrote about how, when she found the courage to leave her husband, she knew that God – whoever and whatever was meant by that word – had strengthened her in her purpose. Her marriage had been destructive and if she had stayed she would have physically or spiritually died. The Archbishop wrote back with courtesy and some sympathy, saying that he had wrestled in anguish with these problems in prayer. But finally he had concluded that 'standards must be maintained'.

To my sister, this phrase was meaningless. What standard was being maintained which allowed the human spirit to be crushed? What spirit of sustaining love – which was her concept of the divine – was nourished by an arid enforcement of a vow taken in a moment of haste and distress?

One of the principal changes of this century has been demographic: we are now living much longer lives than our parents and grandparents. So a marriage that might in earlier centuries have lasted from five to twenty years can now last fifty, sixty, or even seventy. When a young couple make their vow in the words 'till death us do part' or 'so long as we both on earth shall live', what conception can they have of what this involves? When I married at twenty-four, I think my idea of 'forever' was about ten years. Not that I would have said, 'I'll stay with Frank for ten years' but simply that I couldn't envisage anything further ahead. Add to this our growing awareness of the naturalness of sexual feeling towards people of one's own sex, and the recognition that same-sex relationships can be as fulfilling or unfulfilling, as committed or uncommitted, as heterosexual relationships, and we face a situation where insistence on lifelong heterosexual fidelity becomes untenable. We could look at the possibility that an individual may love two people at the same time: making the lifelong commitment to one, planning and sharing life patterns together, while having a deeply loving friendship with another, so that a love that is now seen as infidelity, betrayal, could be seen as something to be adjusted to, rather than as the inevitable end of a lifelong partnership.

There is a point where I have to ask myself: is it my task as a spiritual being, or as a member of a spiritual community, to concern myself with the moral standards of the group, and with giving instruction and warning to others? Or is it my task to delve deep into myself, to concentrate on 'becoming what I am' in H. A. Williams' memorable phrase, on fulfilling my potential and making myself whole, and in doing so open myself responsively to the needs and differences of others?

My rhetorical language shows my personal answer. I take the second course. It involves immense risks. But I go for it, if for no other reason than that it's a task I can do for myself, a task that only I can do. The maintenance of standards involves pressure on others, even oppression of others. The task of becoming what I am is my responsibility, and I am willing to take it, with all the pain and contradiction it involves. It is my step of faith to say that if we all take on this responsibility, then we can relate to each other as whole, entire, rich, strong individuals, one to another, and make up a real spiritual community in which people are loved and let be.

I'll end this chapter with another quotation from *Middlemarch*.

Here is George Eliot's Dorothea, coming to terms at last with the fact that she feels sexual passion for Will Ladislaw. She uses language that we associate with the dark night of the soul as much as with the torments of sexual love: 'In the chill hours of morning light, when all was dim around her, she woke – not with any amazed wondering where she was or what had happened, but with the clearest consciousness that she was looking into the eyes of sorrow . . . She felt as if her soul had been liberated from its terrible conflict; she was no longer wrestling with her grief, but could sit down with it as a lasting companion and make it a sharer in her thoughts.'[16]

INTERVAL

🎵 *On Shadows* 🎵

Good and evil – evil and good. Much of the language of religious discourse starts from this division, this opposition, this struggle. One of my problems is that, when I go into the deepest part of myself, my struggle does not take this form. I can't enter into this dialogue of opposition. I know that I am both good and evil, and when I feel the evil in me I can't deny it or push it away, but walk towards it in my mind, my heart, and ask it what it is and what it means.

What do I mean, walk towards it? I hate evil, fear it, hide from it. When I see violence or calculated destructiveness on film, on television or in the theatre it repels me. I want not only to turn away from it and wash it off me, but want it not to exist, that these destructive people should miraculously see the harm they are doing to others and themselves and on the instant becoming loving and kind. Yet I know there is violence and the destructive impulse in me, or that there has been and could be again. I suspect that the reason I turn away from it is that I fear its existence within me.

A writer friend, Neil Rhodes, wrote in response to my complaint that his characters were too nasty and why couldn't he write about 'pleasant people': 'As for "pleasant people"! Well I haven't met any yet. And if I have (all right, a few) they're much too boring to go in a play. And your people are much too bloody nice! Not a serial killer amongst them.' I wrote in reply: 'Yes, the world is nasty, a lot of it. But some of it is pretty good. . . . I had a fairly vile time as a child, with a lot of ignorant adults foisting their stupidity on to the children in their care instead of taking responsibility for it themselves. But as an adult I've met and loved and been loved by people who have redeemed that. So I know that love is possible and people can grow and change. Why

102

can't this side of the world be portrayed in fiction and drama as well as serial killers? It does exist, and if it's not written about then the mirror we hold up to nature looks back at us and it's Hannibal Lecter.'

To which he responded, patiently, that that's not the point. The point is that whatever the love and goodness in individual people, the world as a whole is a bloody and violent place. From the Moors murderer Ian Brady to the rapists and killers in Bosnia, from the Crusades to the battle over abortion on the streets of a quiet Massachusetts town, people are rejecting, abusing and killing other people. Neil argues that if as writers – as thinkers, reflectors – we present the wholesome side of life only, we're not just presenting a fake world, we're presenting a world in which the goodness cannot be fully seen. If we look to see what light is like, it's the candle in the darkness that will show us, not the equatorial sun at noon. It is Schindler among the Nazis[1] who shows us goodness, because it's against all the odds; or the little servant in the mad world of *Lear* who tries to stop the putting out of Gloucester's eyes and gets run through with a sword for his pains.[2]

I try to resist this argument. If I accept it for a moment – even for long enough to listen to the story of my Ukrainian friend who, at the point of starvation in a World War II labour camp, was given sandwiches by a Nazi guard – I find myself starting to resist it again. To enable myself to grasp it I have to go back to a key experience in my life, one of the most painful and significant experiences, which I keep on forgetting, then remember again, then forget and remember yet again.

When I was about twelve or thirteen some thoroughly nasty books were circulated round the dormitory of my girls' boarding school. The book I chiefly remember was called something like *Secrets of the Nazi Torture Chambers* and described its content in detail, graphically. Each girl read it privately in her 'cubicle' and was allowed a ration of a certain number of days before passing it on to the next girl. Other books of this graphically violent kind were set in other historical periods, like the late Roman Empire, about Nero and Caligula.

I thought, when I started to read about the Nazi torture chambers, that I couldn't bear it. But I did bear it and I read on. I don't know whether I kept the book the prescribed number of days. Time was irrelevant. The impact that it made probably happened within the first few seconds. Because I knew: first, that these things were utterly terrible, the most complete degradation that any human being could ever reach; and, first again (because the insight came concurrently), that *it excited me.*

Years later I read the work of Jung, especially as vividly expressed in Laurens van der Post's combination of biography and personal encounter *Jung and the Story of Our Time,*[3] and found that this man had gone down into the shadowy depths of himself, not knowing whether he would ever come back and realising that he might in fact go mad. Later still I read about George Fox's encounter with 'the natures of those things which were hurtful without, [that they also] were within the hearts and minds of wicked men . . . And I cried unto the Lord, saying, "Why should I be thus, seeing I was never addicted to commit those evils?" And the Lord answered that it was needful that I should have a sense of all conditions . . . and in this I saw the infinite love of God'.[4] More recently still I read Brian Keenan's soul-searing account[5] of his imprisonment and release, not only by and from his violent captors but by and from the contradictions and tensions in the depths of his own finally triumphant personality.

When that book about Nazi atrocities came into my hand, I was an ignorant, sheltered, frightened girl at the start of puberty. I had little or no awareness of the historical forces that had shaped themselves into Nazism or of the psychological forces that lead human beings to draw degradation on to themselves and their victims. All I knew was the story and the impact it made on me. I knew the pornography of violence.

But at the same time as this ignorance, there existed in me a different kind of awareness. I was aware that this was evil. No denying that. But equally undeniable was that, if it excited me, this evil must also be *in me.* And then – a huge leap, this, but one I made readily – that if it is in me, probably

104

it is in most people. And if evil was in me and in other people – and this was ultimately the most important thing – then it was vital for me to remember that fact, even when I loathed it and rejected it and wanted to shout from the mountain tops that it wasn't the case. I knew that such remembrance was necessary for my healing, a part of my wholeness.

I couldn't possibly have articulated it in this way at the time. But I don't think that I've mistaken the essence, or that I express it incorrectly now. This was the core of my insight. It was horrible, and true, and wonderful. It made me understand Yeats' phrase when I came across it: 'a terrible beauty'.[6] That the knowledge of evil should be a vital part of wholeness: what more seismic insight could there be? What could be farther away from the innocence of the Garden of Eden before the apple was touched? What less capable of expression and absorption, at any age, in any state of knowledge or ignorance? I've returned to it again and again in my consciousness, and in a small way have written about it.[7] Mostly it stays at the back of my mind. But if it ever starts to slip away, if I try to deny it, something makes me re-cognise it and cling on to it with dogged deliberateness.

Recently, with good counselling and the love of my friends, I've been able to look more closely at what goes on in the deeper parts of my psyche and my soul. Some of the fear of what lies there has slipped away. Without that love, without the support and insights and challenge of friends and of my spiritual community, I don't know what would have become of that hidden side of me. When people ask, on some day of terrible news, 'How can people *commit* these atrocities?', I often join in the chorus, and I really mean what I'm saying. Yet at some more fundamental level I know that given the circumstances, given deprivation and humiliation and suggestion and degradation and fear, I could probably be drawn into committing almost any act imaginable.

Such knowledge sets judgement aside. And the paradox is that, as a writer, my besetting temptation is to judge my characters, while at the same time I know I mustn't, I must stay inside them whatever they do and say and think. So comes the tension in my argument with Neil about violence in plays. The tension is increased by the way we in our culture, in any culture, use individuals and groups as symbols: Mother Teresa versus Myra Hindley. It's made more problematic by the way all writers must use symbolism to convey their meaning in poetry, prose and drama. Even while I've been writing this chapter I've been aware of my use of the word 'Nazi' to convey the ultimate in evil. Yet the finest writers can overcome even this, like Shakespeare, like C. P. Taylor in his play *Good*, which shows devastatingly how a reasonably good man can gradually, inexorably, become a fascist.[8] Adolf Hitler sits in our cultural awareness as the incarnation of evil. But the Treaty of Versailles was also evil in its intentions and its effects. So was the anti-Semitism rife in Britain, Poland, Czechoslovakia and the Soviet Union in the 1930s, and which existed before, and exists now. Every destructive act has causes which were destructive in different and often unseen ways.

But what about the psychopathic killer whose motivation seems beyond the normal sequence of cause and effect, whose actions seem to come directly from an unquestionable, almost inhuman and therefore perhaps outside force of evil? I have no answer to that except the answer of faith – 'One day we will know the reasons' – or the pragmatic answer – 'Hard cases make bad argument, and prevent me taking the wider argument into account'.

I've known two people who have killed another human being. One was a woman, one was a man. One killed in war, the other killed in extreme circumstances. One spent the rest of a lifetime working to prevent the circumstances happening again, the other lived an average life unnoticed in the suburbs. One struggled with self-abasement and fear and found it impossible to go on living, the other died of illness after living to a good age.

The one who couldn't go on living felt a sense of judgement on what had happened, a personal, inward condemnation as well as the condemnation of society. I recently saw a play which showed as the central character someone in similar circumstances, which told the story as to a friend so that the audience could understand it. The character entered our imaginations in such a way that we knew we could have been that person and could have done that deed. All the other characters – police, legal representatives, doctors – used words of judgement to label and condemn. I could hear them condemning my friend in the same terms.

I'm aware of the words that could be used to condemn me at this point: 'sympathising with the perpetrator rather than the victim', 'letting emotion cloud the judgement', 'breaching the very fabric of a safe society'. And I know that those words of condemnation are valid.

But I also know that my spiritual life demands a movement towards interconnectedness. It pushes me in the direction of knowing my connectedness with all people and with all natural things. That is the direction of love. The language of judgement puts a brake on my movement towards love.

Judgement is my self-protection. If I didn't protect myself I would go under. I need my limits. I feel my limits and, when I'm able to love, the love pushes against the limits and expands them a little. Then there's the opposite move-ment: I'm afraid and draw back and put up barriers of judgement again. But when I'm ready and when the love pours in like grace, I can allow the limits to expand again. There's no logic to the times or circumstances when con-straint or expansion come. It's an ebb and flow, a breathing in and breathing out, an alternation of states of being that seems necessary to the process. I can't expand all the time. I've got to go inwards and be still in my fear. I've got to be still, inside my complicated self, with all my love and imagination and lack of imagination and struggles with love. The physical world, the phases of the moon, the cycle of the seasons, the rhythm of the tides, the growth and death of plants and trees, hold endless metaphors for this process of tension and alternation.

'Tension' – 'contradiction' – 'paradox'. These are the words I reach for instead of 'division' and 'opposition'. I try to forbid myself the words 'good' and 'evil' in the sense of two forces inhabiting different psychological or spiritual worlds. To me they belong in the same world, the same mind and heart; the world and mind and heart that I inhabit myself, that inhabits me. To use the concept of evil is to refuse to admit that I can't cope with what has happened, with what caused it to happen, and with my complicity with those causes as a member of society and a tiny part in a vast world. The concept externalises. It projects on to others what I'm afraid might be lurking in myself.

If I can find a principle in all this, it is that when we condemn people, we condemn them to stay as they are and we condemn our understanding to stay as it is. We condemn ourselves and them to stay within the limits of this moment. But if we make the huge effort involved in moving towards people, we open up the possibility that they may change, and that we might change in our understanding; that our moral universe might shift a little, might widen and deepen; that we ourselves might spiritually grow.

It's hard. It's so hard to keep the attention focused. I want so much to put a label on the person and turn away. I find that as I've been writing this my mind has slithered on to other things. My feelings have pulled me away, literally: they've wrenched me from the word-processor and from the thought sequences because the whole matter is so painful.

'An honest religious thinker is a tightrope walker,' said Wittgenstein. 'He almost looks as though he were walking on nothing but air.'[9] If we let go of judgement, we also let go of the conviction that we can, by sheer force of will, bring about good in the world. This is the tightrope we walk on. This is the abyss we look down into. If we base our love on the principle of ever-widening understanding – if the reality and the shadow are never divided – then we don't know where our boundaries are. We can't define good and evil as absolutes any more. One element in the phrase *I believe in God* can be expanded as *I believe that good will finally triumph over evil*. From where I stand, especially having faced the possibility of the world blowing itself up in nuclear holocaust or poisoning itself by environmental disaster, there seems no real evidence to support the belief that good will triumph. It may be that humankind, through aggressiveness or mere thoughtlessness, will bring life on this planet to an abrupt or painfully long-drawn-out close. If we accept that, we are truly looking down from the tightrope into the abyss.

That is desolate. Yet, if I cling to the old language of

opposites, I risk sliding into the sort of hypocrisy and sentimentality that have been the hallmarks of Christianity since
the Victorian era. I once wrote: 'Christianity's sweetness 'n'
light is deeply depressing, because depression comes from
knowledge denied. Generalised optimism – "God/good will
prevail" – "We know what's good for you" – is suffused
with the Will to Power. It demands submission, dependence,
childish acceptance. After Auschwitz, after Lockerbie, it's
essential that humankind grows up.'[10]

The words Good and Evil come from an old world view,
from a world in which God and the Devil fought over our
souls and divided the spoils between them. I'm struggling
towards a different mental framework: one that uses the
language of understanding to replace the language of condemnation; that includes awareness of psychological complexity, of the pressures that society and the mass media and
the structures of power put upon us; that accepts the intricacy
of cause-and-effect patterns, the interconnectedness of all
things, even the connection between creativity and destruction. It takes all my courage. The shadows play over my
consciousness and I want to run from the struggle. But
something tells me that in judging other people I judge
myself, and in using judgement, in using the language of
opposition, I limit myself and I limit the spirit within me.
The other way is growth and discovery, wherever that will
lead.

> Jesus said, 'If you bring forth what is within you, what
> you bring forth will save you. If you do not bring forth
> what is within you, what you do not bring forth will
> destroy you.'
>
> (*Gospel according to Thomas* 45:29–33[11])

7

HEALINGS AND LEADINGS

As you look into this being's eyes, let yourself
become aware of the powers that are there . . . Consider what these untapped powers can do for the
healing of our planet and the relishing of our
common life . . . As you consider that, let yourself
become aware of your desire that this person be free
from hatred, free from greed, free from sorrow and
the causes of suffering . . . Know that what you are
now experiencing is the great loving-kindness.

(JOANNA ROGERS MACY, *Despair and Power
in the Nuclear Age*[1])

When I was a mother of two young children I got to know an
old man called Gilbert. Gilbert was a healer. He discovered that
he had the gift of healing when he was a child. His brother had
injured a leg in childhood play and Gilbert on an impulse laid his
hand on the wound. His hand felt warm, and the leg quickly and
spontaneously healed.

He was shocked by the incident and too frightened to try the
experiment again. As a young adult, though, he began to know
that he shouldn't deny it and used his healing powers quietly when
it seemed to be appropriate. He never doubted that the power
was there and that it was the power of God, available to him for
channelling to others. The only question was whether he was
willing to use it. He resisted putting it to full use until he was in
his fifties when he took the plunge, gave up his job and threw
himself on the goodness of God and of the people he offered to
help. He found himself a small room in a house near where he
lived, told his patients that he depended on their good will for his
bread, and trusted. He had a fund of stories of how he was often
near to bankruptcy when a large cheque came to save the day.

Many of his patients, he said, had come to him with no faith of their own and as a last resort: 'It's a load of cobblers but I'll try anything.' This made no difference. He healed people who were faithless and faithful, who were present and absent, who were sick in body or in spirit.

We knew him towards the end of his life, when the gift of healing was no longer so readily available to him. But I had no doubt at all that his account of his life's work was trustworthy in every particular, and this came as a surprise to me because I would have described myself as a sceptic where questions of spiritual healing were concerned. As a girl I had written to one of the school's visiting clergymen to ask whether he thought faith healing might help my mother, and the reply was full of warnings about delving into this dangerous area. When Gilbert joined the Society of Friends in his eighties it was the first religious body he had ever made a commitment to, though there could have been no one with a stronger or more mainstream faith, because he had found the churches either nervous of or hostile to the whole subject of healing.

But for me it was not the attitude of the religious mainstream that was the main hurdle. It was my sense of justice. In terms of a God-out-there, the question was: if the Almighty was so concerned for our health, why did He need my or anyone else's prayers to prevail on Him to bring it about? Worse, why was He so partial in His favours? In less realist, more Sea-of-Faith terms: why should one person be healed and another not simply because one of them was coincidentally in the neighbourhood of someone who had 'the gift'? When pushed, I would remember what I'd been taught as a child: that healing was something wonderful that happened in Jesus' day, by Jesus' agency and the apostles in the spirit of Jesus, that we must revere the stories told within the pages of the Bible but we mustn't assume they were relevant to our time or that such powers were available to us now. I wondered at the discrepancy between then and now and concluded that it was part of the chasm in mind-set between a religion-based, pre-scientific era and our age of sceptical materialism.

I would walk on sunny days with my two small daughters up the hill to where Gilbert lived with his daughter and sit in the garden with him while the children played, plaguing him with these questions. I can't remember what his answers were; I didn't listen too attentively because I knew I couldn't accept them anyway. But I loved him, he was a friend to the whole family, and I respected what he did and what he was. On a Sunday at Quaker Meeting he would often stand to speak about the omniscience, omnipotence and omnipresence of God, shaking the back of your chair if you happened to be sitting in front of him. I alternated between two positions on this: finding that I could accept his language because, though it was alien to me, I knew that it was the natural expression of Gilbert's faith, and fury that he had the sort of total conviction, almost proof, of God's existence and healing power that was denied to me. Gilbert himself helped me to balance these two positions by listening patiently when I expressed my doubts.

Where healing was concerned, I found that I was now part of a community who accepted the language of healing as part of ordinary discourse. A number of Quakers whose opinions I respected took it for granted that healing was there for the asking if you were spiritually open. It might not come in the dramatic ways that Gilbert described, though occasionally it did. Again I took these stories on board in argumentative spirit, alternately cross and grateful to have my cussedness challenged.

Gilbert told other stories about people being saved from extraordinary dangers by the power of prayer. I opted for the attitude of Don Cupitt[2] about such miracles: it's fine for the aircrash survivor to thank God for deliverance, but what about those who were killed? Where was God for them? Where was the value of their lives for us?

I could accept more easily the kind of healing, not necessarily by drugs or surgery, that was given us by medical staff. For instance, the midwife who delivered our first baby was near to retirement but open to new methods. She came along to some of my natural childbirth classes to learn what I was learning, and respected my wishes about home delivery and the minimal use of drugs. This wasn't spiritual healing in the ordinary sense, but it helped to pave the way for me to cope with the pain of childbirth and for us to be confident and loving parents. Similarly, I remember a GP coming to see our fretful tiny baby, holding her quietly on his knee while asking us gentle questions about her health and progress till she was asleep and we were calm. I've seen this again and again: the ability of confident, caring nurses and doctors to draw healing resources from within the patients themselves.

Gilbert died as he lived, in total faith. He had been longing to go for some time and wondered what the Almighty was waiting for. His daughter and her family were on an exchange visit to an American university and he went to stay with a friend whom he trusted. One evening he asked her, 'Would you mind if I died in your house?' She said, smiling, 'Not in the least. Go ahead, enjoy yourself.' Next morning she knocked on his door to ask if he'd like an early cup of tea and found that he had died in the night. I knew that his spirit had chosen to leave his body and felt pretty certain, too, that it was now wherever he had longed for it to be.

Openness to suffering

At the same time my internal arguments went on. I believed in the scientific order, in the laws of cause and effect. I couldn't see, and still can't see, how the natural world might operate effectively if the cause-and-effect sequence is broken at will. And I would often be struck by a kind of rage at the suffering that could not be healed. The specific question *Why me? Why them?* has for some reason bothered me less than it bothers many people. The world is so full of suffering, so beset by contingency and accident, that to demand reasons for each individual pain could easily drive you to madness. But the pain of witnessing the suffering of people I cared for drove me to despair. So I tried to protect myself from it.

I became a creative writing tutor for a group of people with cerebral palsy, and for the first time I longed to have the gift of healing myself. If only I could take each one of them by the hand, untwist their limbs, open their mouths to speak and lead them, walking, from their wheelchairs! Some of them went on trips to Lourdes. One went again and again and enjoyed herself hugely with a gang of friends, while another refused to go a second time, disillusioned that he'd come back in the same physical state as he went.

One day Val, one of the most physically disabled of the group, found the courage to read a portion of her life story (or to have it read at her instigation) to the rest of the group. 'When I was born, I was ordinary ... When I was four I got meningitis. I remember feeling on fire, my head being hit by hammers, my legs no longer there, wanting to be sick. Then there were the dreams, the nightmares . . . I seemed to be alone in that little white walled room for days and nights before my parents came to see me . . . After I was six Mum took me home. It was hard. Barbara could walk and talk and I felt angry. There was also the baby.'[3] I was moved by her courage in articulating such loss and pain, both acute and chronic, and realised that I had closed myself off from her suffering until then. Now that I'd opened up there was no way of closing the door again. It hurt me to feel it and I wanted it to stop hurting, just as Val wanted it to stop hurting and couldn't stop it either. I could distract myself by being busy with other things, but she couldn't. All she could do was find the courage to find the words.

But I knew that sometimes I still needed to shut myself off, to barricade myself. As with questions of good, evil, love and judgement, life would be impossible if I was always open. But it would be impoverished if I was always closed.

This is a tension that is still unresolved. But Val, in offering the reality of her suffering, had offered me a kind of healing. What she wrote and what she was, day by day, deepened my experience of what life could be. She would become electric with the power of her feeling: grief, pleasure at sunshine, eagerness, desperation. Sometimes the power was blocked and would leak out intermittently, stutteringly, as if in Morse code. Sometimes she wanted to switch off the current. Then doggedly she'd switch it back on again and stand in the flashes of lightning, exhausted, shining. She increased my power of understanding. She expanded my ability to love.

Gradually, under the ice-cap of intellectual argument, something was melting. I was shifting. One day I was present at a talk on spiritual healing. I found I could actually listen to it without rehearsing the old hostile arguments in my head. The speaker said that everyone has the ability to heal and be healed, that healing energy exists to be drawn upon. Just as most of us, if helped, can pick out a few notes on a piano but an occasional gifted person gives their all to it and becomes a concert pianist, so some people treasure the gift of healing within themselves and give their all to it. If they concentrate on transmitting healing energy to someone who is ill, it can replace the ill person's depleted energy and turn around the body's movement towards sickness into a movement towards renewed health.

So I opened myself to this possibility. With a rush of passionate mid-life energy came the breaking of the ice and the movement forward. Nothing outwardly dramatic took place, but there was a loosening of inner twists, a shifting of old bitterness. I became aware that I could be healed and could bring about healing in myself and others, not necessarily by the laying on of hands or by a circle of prayer, but by being there, by willing my energies in that direction, by being open, by letting life flow and occasionally surge through me, unblocked and free.

God's will, or the right way

I sense that I have been frozen over too on the question of the 'guidance of God', but that here as well, under the solid surface, something is moving.

Religious people have always talked about God 'leading' them, that they are 'called', that they have 'discovered God's will'. Since the night at Hilary's bedside when I was eight I've distrusted that language. What kind of a Being would send anguish and loss for our or someone else's edification, would weigh up our needs against someone else's needs and conclude that ours – or theirs – are of no consequence? How do you know you are led or guided or called? Are you sure it isn't self-deception, that you aren't using God out of a need for certainty, or to give you extra clout in the argument? How is it possible to discern the will of God? Does such a will exist; is there a Being who has a Plan, an intention that each of us should behave in a certain way? If there is, what does that say about our free will and that of the people around us? God as the great Puppeteer disappeared from my view decades ago, along with the realisation that God can be either all-powerful or all-loving but not both. But the same arguments still present themselves to me in non-God language: in terms of 'asking for help' in discerning 'the right way' or 'the way forward'. Often it seems impossible to decide what is right. My own strength, the ordinary power of human discernment, doesn't seem adequate to the task. There are times when the pressure of events seems to force a decision to act in a way that's almost against my will. That seems like some kind of 'calling'.

In the early 1980s a small number of women with courage and insight about the nuclear arms issue formed a local Women for Peace group. I was asked if I'd join, but resisted because I hate campaigning, leafleting and marching. My role in life was different, I thought. It was to support people, to talk things through with them when they needed and send them back renewed.

But in the end I had to join. Inch by inch, resisting all the way, I got more and more involved. It seemed a necessity. It felt like cleaning up shit: someone has to do it. I could see the death of the world as I saw it at the time of the Cuba crisis but magnified a hundred times. For brief, terrible moments I could see the annihilation of nations and individuals as clearly as I could see the rain outside the kitchen or the goods in a shop window. It was intolerable. Campaigning, marching, leafleting might not change the destructive course of world leaders, but it was what I could do and I had to do it. Nadezhda Mandelstam wrote that if all you can do is scream, then you must scream.[4]

The Women for Peace group grew, and in the summer of 1983 we planned a march to the Cruise Missile base at Greenham Common for Hiroshima Day, August 6th. It would coincide, in the shape of a star, with other women's groups from all over the country and would take a fortnight. I could only do part of the march because of other commitments, but eventually I said I would go. We were to take the younger children with us in an old bus, which would also carry our bedding and minimal luggage, but we would rely for roof and food on local women's and peace groups along the way. An all-woman television crew took up our story and filmed us as we made plans, set out, and walked.

It was a recipe for stress, and as such it worked. When we finally got to Greenham we heard from other women about the inspiring and cohesive weeks they'd had on the road – stories which reduced me to silence, because our road as I'd experienced it had been fraught with conflict. Some of the group wanted to smoke, others wanted no smoking. The proportions of carnivorous and vegetarian food were never right. Some wanted to shout slogans as we walked and to approach local communities in combative spirit to argue our case; others wanted to give out a quiet peaceful image and leave the banners to do the rest. Dancing and singing were a witness for life on earth, said some; others were embarrassed by display. I hated arguing the anti-nuclear case; I got far too emotional. Many of the stopping places were at Forces' establishments where we were to meet personnel and press and where the bombers thundered overhead to remind us of the horrors we were opposing. I forgot all the statistics I'd learnt, the cogent arguments I'd been rehearsing and the principles of peaceful exchange. I wanted simply to screech, 'Do you *want* the world to end in nuclear holocaust, then?' On these public occasions we managed to keep up a reasonably civilised front. But at night, overwhelmed by the presence of such horror so close, we split into bitter factions.

I was a feminist and a pacifist, and here I was amongst women fighting. I was one of the fighters. Some managed to stay above the conflict and were simply grateful for the kindness we met on the way, but I was not one of them. Why had I been 'called'? So that my aggression and fear could be dug out of safe bunkers and exposed to other women? If there was a plan, this didn't seem part of it.

Reflecting from the distance of years later, the experience still seems like something I had to go through. At the very least it taught me some of the stubborn skill of 'face the fear and do it anyway'. On the last night before we got to Greenham we camped in the garden of a sympathiser on the northern side of the Downs. Rumours flew that some young thugs had spotted us as a soft target. I didn't sleep, my muscles ached and my blisters hurt. I was tempted to fold up my tiny old tent, hitch to Newbury and catch the mail train home. It was probably a different kind of cowardice that kept me there: the fear of facing the other women when they got back from Greenham and asked me why I hadn't seen it through.

But there were unexpected moments of vision and grace. At one small demonstration I stood in the centre of town with my placard. The few of us there decided that our vigil would be a silent one, and I experienced one of my moments of knowledge. It came as an awareness that the deaths of Jesus and of Gandhi and Martin Luther King were, if not of their own choosing and willing, the essence of their being, the meaning of their message and lives. They went to their deaths because if they'd fought with weapons for what they believed in they would have denied what they stood for. If they clung on to the Spirit, believing that they were its only human vehicle, they would lose that very Spirit; whereas if they let it go, it would survive. *Only* by letting it go could they allow it to survive.

So I knew there was no point in 'fighting for peace'. Such a war would be a crusade, killing what it was supposed to promote. The Spirit can seem to be lost when an individual person or cause is lost. But that person or cause is only part of the Spirit. Those who follow a person or a cause sometimes have to let it go and trust that the Spirit will live again in some other form.

This insight echoed one I'd felt years earlier, watching the Chester Cycle of Mystery Plays acted out by local people on the Cathedral Green. I watched the disciples quarrelling as they sat down for their last meal with Jesus, and I wanted to leap on to the set and shout to him, 'Watch it! They'll let you down! Don't trust them! Save yourself!' At the same time I realised that he wouldn't save himself. That wasn't what he was living for. That was why he preferred to die. He was compelled to trust that what he stood for would survive even though he himself did not.

My embattled stance against the Jesus of endless sermons began to evaporate. I'd felt the experience of a moment in Jesus' life. It wasn't everyone's view of Jesus' meaning, but it came to me clearly and has shone a light for me since.

In the years after the Peace Movement I got involved in party politics, and this was an arena where I saw clearly the disjunction between ends and means. The end that I and others were working for was a more just and communally responsive society. But the means we were offered was combative, adversarial. One side or individual had to lose in order for the other to win. It seemed a means completely inappropriate in spirit to its end, and the feeling grew in me that the spiritual was an essential basis for the political. I can't see how this could come about but I'm certain that it's a question that needs to be articulated and addressed. If we need greater political literacy, we also need a spiritual literacy to back it up, to inform it.

I have been so aware of my tendency to be conned, and to deceive myself, that I've nourished in myself a sceptical reaction to most things. I have been, and still am, resistant to notions of 'leadings' and 'guidance'. Yet I feel the pressure of new ways of being. New ways offer themselves and I turn away; they offer themselves again and I notice; and then at last I take real notice, and move. The first move is generally small and requires me only to say, 'Tell me more'. Sometimes my resistance is enormous, as with the peace movement. Sometimes the new takes me by surprise, as with my attitudes to love and sexuality. Sometimes it's an on-going process, like my relationship with the movements that come under the heading Human Potential or the Age of Aquarius. Sometimes it's a slow, gentle motion, unnoticed or ignored, like the change that happened in me over healing. I vary enormously in my attitude to change, and the variations don't seem to have any logical basis in the circumstances of the time. So I have to monitor my openness to change, and expand it where I can.

Forgiveness

During my years as a Christian I wrestled with the concept of forgiveness. Linked as it was with the vision of myself as a corrupt and stupid child, it was a baby that I gladly threw out with the bath-water of self-abasement. I took a look at the language of power and submission and began to ditch the whole edifice of sin and forgiveness as part of that unwholesome emotional structure. If I'd experienced forgiveness it was not as absolution or amnesty so much as a grace, in the sense that Paul Tillich described it: 'Grace strikes us when we are in great pain or restlessness . . . Sometimes at that moment a wave of light breaks into our darkness, and it is as though a voice were saying: "You are accepted." '[5]

This left unresolved the question of my own forgiveness of other people. I'd realised that if I disliked someone, or found myself unable to cope with their difficulties, I could sometimes come round into love and acceptance if I simply let it ride and waited. But this left untouched the more significant instances when someone had specifically wronged me. One particular injury I carried round with me for years. I knew the motive behind it, which was understandable, but the person concerned didn't seem aware of the wrong, or at any rate didn't apologise for it. I'd had other breaches of relationship healed by a heart-felt apology, but that seemed impossible in this instance. So I willed myself not to do any reciprocal injury and to talk about it only to those whom I could trust to discipline themselves not to pass on my hostility. But I was bearing resentment like a burden, and it was heavy. I knew it was injuring me more than the original injury had done. I saw the person only as someone who could injure. I set aside other people's love and admiration of the same individual, wondering at it, rejecting it as misconceived.

Eventually, I found I had forgiven. How? When I read Marge Piercy's poem, 'How divine is forgiving?' I leapt on it as a key:

> We forgive mostly not from strength
> but through imperfections, for memory
> wears transparent as a glass with the pattern
> washed off, till we stare past what injured us.
> We forgive because we too have done
> the same to others easy as a mudslide;
> or because anger is a fire that must be fed
> and we are too tired to rise and haul a log.[6]

It came through waiting, and through trust that forgiveness would at long last come about. Something had forbidden me to say 'I will never forgive'. I left open a small crack of hope that one day the burden would just slip off my shoulders. And it did. I couldn't even say exactly when it slipped. But it had gone. There came an occasion when I had to undergo one of those uncomfortable encounters, and the feeling of resentment was not there.

Maybe I can forgive when I feel that I am forgiven, or to use Tillich's language, I can accept because I am accepted.

As I write that, I see immediately the connection between the word *accept* and the word *respect*. Acceptance is a reciprocal thing, just as respect has to be reciprocal. When I am with people I love and trust in an atmosphere of equality and acceptance, there's no question of the self-conscious humility and self-abasement demanded by an imposed request for absolution. The fearful struggle against sin becomes a slow, disciplined search for clarity and the willingness to change. A perspective begins to dawn in which it becomes clearer what is gold in me and what is dross. Slowly I find the capacity to let go a little of the dross, or even find the insight that acceptance of the dross – or the shit, or even the fire of hate – is a necessary part of the way. As grit is essential to the production of the pearl, so tension is necessary to the motion forward.

Building a spiritual community

Gradually, through this personal account, I've been moving from the individual journey towards the concept of a community where the idiosyncratic individual can feel at home and be able to grow. The words I've just written, about being 'with people I love and trust in an atmosphere of equality and acceptance', are at the heart of this movement from one stage to the next.

It seems to me that if we are to form a spiritual community that cherishes and nurtures the freedom of its individual members, then the principles on which it is based must be the same as the principles on which the personal journey is based: love, trust, equality, acceptance, respect.

What do I mean by 'equality'? Clearly, being equal doesn't mean being identical. The struggle for an identical voice means the silencing of the uncomfortable, perhaps visionary, idiosyncratic voice. Equality means the acceptance of difference. In fact it means the celebration of difference as a source of enrichment. So it must mean *equality of validity*. That is the point at which acceptance turns into respect.

A spiritual community doesn't need to be a church. It could be a group of friends who meet to talk about their spiritual journeys. It could be a creative listening group, a story-telling group, a meditation or yoga class. It might or might not define itself as a spiritual community. The community or spirituality may simply exist in the minds and hearts of the members. The defining factors are respect for themselves and each other in the pursuit and account of their spiritual journeys, together with a certain loyalty of commitment so that they are open and available to each other.

Recurring themes so far have been *experience, depth*, and *trust*. If people are to commit themselves to a spiritual community, it's vital that they experiment with trust and that the experiment usually pays off. The experiment will involve telling the truth, and it will pay off if what is said is believed and if confidentiality is respected. Telling the truth will involve digging beyond quick reactions and superficial memories to find insights and patterns and connections. The pay-off will be a quality of listening that honours the insights and doesn't try to belittle or cap them. The basis of it all will be a sharing of real experience in all its opacity, complexity and muddle, with the pay-off that no judgements are dealt out to deny or condemn it, that no one jumps to hasty conclusions about its deep meaning, but everyone waits for the truth to emerge in the individual's own time.

A word that has cropped up increasingly is 'discipline'. This is an odd concept to find in a book dedicated to freedom of expression in the spiritual life. But I'm more and more certain that discipline is a necessary tool for the journey.

For instance, where injury and forgiveness are concerned. Marge Piercy says that 'anger is a fire that must be fed'. But it needn't only be weariness that stops us feeding the fire. It can be self-discipline. Similarly, in a group setting, each individual needs to exercise self-discipline in the recognition of other people's right to speak and be heard, and in truly listening to what they say, however strange or uncongenial it might be.

This is especially true where group decision-making is concerned. In the hierarchical and adversarial society of the West we get little or no training in joint decision-making. Armed with the philosophy of 'If I'm right, you must be wrong', we set out to work, to make partnerships and to bring up children. A spiritual community can be a place to experiment with a more creative way of making decisions. It can be a practice ground for listening, for taking other people's feelings and opinions on board and trying to find a way that meets everyone's needs. I find it helpful to learn from management training methods that develop 'win-win' as opposed to 'win-lose' ways of making decisions. In *Getting to Yes*,[7] the classic work on this theme, Roger Fisher and William Ury point to the fact that a sense of belonging, recognition, and ability to have control over one's life are basic human needs. When we recognise those needs in the person we're arguing or bargaining with, we're far more likely to reach a mutually acceptable solution. Since my instinct is to use a spiritual vocabulary, I would identify those three needs as spiritual as well as human. Others would go further and say that, when a 'win-win' solution is reached, we've experienced the guidance of God. But as always I'm sceptical about God-language, on the alert for the kind of mind-set illustrated by this probably apocryphal remark: 'Don't trouble me with the facts, I'm listening to the Holy Spirit.'

I remember an occasion in a Quaker business meeting where we had to make an especially difficult decision. A member who was recently divorced wanted to re-marry. Her ex-husband still lived nearby and was extremely hurt, first by his wife's departure and doubly by her rapid re-marriage. The people at the business meeting were divided. The new couple could easily have married in a Registry Office, and some thought they should just have done that. There was a strong feeling for the abandoned husband's hurt; to give the new marriage a blessing would add unnecessary pain. Others were glad that the woman and her new partner wanted a spiritual ceremony to mark this new relationship and thought we should look to the future. The arguments went to and fro. I felt sympathy first with one side and then the other, tossed about, not knowing which way up I would land.

When the pros and cons had been established and the complex feelings on both sides acknowledged, someone pointed out that we too, as friends and members of the same community, had been hurt by the break-up of the original marriage. It disturbed our expectations of equilibrium. It forced us to abandon assumptions and to be willing to live with uncertainty and different patterns of relationship. We also felt the burden of the ex-husband's pain, and some of us didn't know how to handle it.

This brought a release. People stopped saying what they thought should happen, and began to say where they themselves were coming from. Someone articulated passionately a sense of guilt. How could that original couple have been heading for divorce without any of us even knowing that things were going wrong? Someone else said how helpless they felt about the whole situation. Others gave moving accounts of their own experience of divorce or re-marriage or the decision to remain single.

We decided to allow the new marriage, but at the same time to give especially sensitive care to the man who was wounded by the new situation. Acknowledging what we felt, opening ourselves to our own pain, had made us able to see more clearly what to do with the specific problem in front of us.

Opening to each other in a group, and finding creative ways of being together and moving forward, will be the subject of the next chapter.

8

TRANSFORMING ME INTO US

[In the ceremony of *hoquet*] the individual notes of
any melodic line are ascribed to individual singers,
so that no one singer carries the entire melody but
each carries an essential part of it and all are therefore
equally necessary.

(COLIN TURNBULL, '*Liminality*'[1])

I have been talking about language in a spiritual context, not in
the sense of a language we can all use together but in the sense of
searching for a way that we can communicate spiritually one with
another. That has inevitably meant looking at the relationships we
have with each other: power relationships, love relationships,
relationships that require space for individual freedom and that
require a meeting of minds for making decisions and helping each
other to grow.

What I have learnt about a language for my spiritual journey is
that, though I may articulate my journey in different words from
those that other people find for theirs, the differences can co-exist.
There may be occasions for speaking the same words together, but
the basis is a search for the words that each of us can use authenti-
cally. An essential component is the respect that we have both for
our own words as they emerge and for the words of others. The
search for words turns out to be a search for our identity as
individual human beings, and for authentic relationships in community. It requires both that we speak our truth and that we're
heard, and that we listen to other truths and take them on board
in a spirit of acceptance. It is, at heart, about being honest and
being receptive.

Making decisions

Honesty and receptivity are qualities that are the building-blocks of community. But, as well as a philosophy, communities need to develop practical ways of being together.

When we think of 'community' we often think of particular communities: groups of people who have opted to live together in larger forms than the nuclear family so that they can work out different ways of managing their economy, their life-styles and their ways of bringing up children. Some communities, like the traditional monastic house, have a hierarchical decision-making structure. Others, including some of the more radical religious orders, have developed ways of decision-making that don't involve an authority passing down edicts from above. But it is often over decision-making that communities founder.

In our wider 'democratic' society in Britain we have devolved much of our decision-making – or have had it devolved for us – into the hands of those we appoint once every three, four of five years and over whom we then have no control. We live in a society where some people's needs, usually the needs of the most vulnerable, are judged inimical to the needs of the community at large – where we 'can't afford' the care of the elderly or the long-term sick, or the proper education of children. It may be, at the time I'm writing, that we've reached the bottom of the pit of this philosophy and that a new realisation is dawning that the fulfilment of each human being contributes to the fulfilment of the organism of society as a whole. I hope so. But clearly in our corporate political life we haven't found ways to treat each person as of equal value.

At the centre of what I've been writing is a vision of a community who find ways of being together that enable them to share the spiritual depth of each other's lives and allow individual truth to enrich the whole. Treating each individual as ultimately valuable is the basis of any spiritual community. How can such a community develop decision-making processes that ensure that every individual is valued and their truth heard?

Carol worked in a large organisation. She occupied a senior position, the only woman to do so. Despite the stated policy of the organisation she was paid on a lower salary than men in a similar position. She needed to take the case to a tribunal, but the situation had weakened her confidence so much that she didn't feel strong enough to do it; in any case, she knew that it would make her position at work even more difficult. She felt there were wider issues at stake than her own salary, but other women colleagues were afraid of getting involved. She didn't know whether to go ahead or not. To Carol, there was a moral imperative to struggle for justice. But maybe she should cultivate forgiveness?

Then she learnt about 'meetings for discernment', or 'clearness groups'. Several different religious groups, including her own, had started to use these as a way of helping people to make difficult decisions. It might be appropriate before a marriage; or during the break-up of a marriage, to decide about finances or the care of the children; or to help understand whether a vocation is a true one or not.

The process of 'clearness' or 'discernment' involves four to six people from the church or spiritual community, some who are close to the individual and some not. They spend an evening concentrating on the problem in quite a disciplined and formal way. They may start and end with a period of silence, to focus the mind and inform the quality of the listening. The aim is not to make a decision on the individual's behalf, or even help them come to a decision at that time. It is to support them, to reflect the problem back together with various possible solutions, so that it can be seen more clearly and more as a whole.

Carol emerged from her clearness group confident that she was good at her job, that she had the right to defend her own and other women's position as equals in the workplace, and that as the case went ahead she'd be able to call on this group of people, who knew her and cared about her and whom she trusted, to talk things through and regain strength. She was transformed.

That process of group support is helpful for individual decision-making. If a group itself needs to make decisions, there is a way of helping people to listen carefully and sympathetically, even to the more uncomfortable and unwelcome contributions. It involves a 'conch'. The concept originated in the native American culture. It was articulated in English by William Golding in *Lord of the Flies*, where boys stranded on a remote island bring discipline to their group meetings by allowing someone to speak only when they hold an object designated as special for this purpose, in their case a conch shell. A 'conch' can actually be anything – a feather, a pebble, a marble egg, a toy. Sometimes it's called a talking stick. It can be put in the centre of a circle or passed from hand to hand. Using this special object ensures that everyone can have their say on the question at issue. No one is allowed to interrupt, and if someone thinks that a time of reflection is needed – maybe a period of calm in a stormy argument – they can simply hold the conch in silence.

The conch method can be used in any small spiritual group simply as a way of encouraging people to listen to each other in depth. An individual can hold it for as long as they would like the silence to last, either before or after they speak or instead of speaking.

These quiet and careful ways of being together during a process of making decisions imply a degree of trust that isn't always present in a community, however spiritual it intends to be. It's possible to misuse a group for clearness or discernment, to try to press the person concerned to act in the way others feel is right rather than in the way that's right for them. People can misuse the conch, holding it not to create quiet reflection but to prevent other people speaking, or to speak for too long and off the point. There may even come a time when the group is torn by conflict and, whatever methods they use to try to listen to each other and bring healing, there is no way to save it from falling apart. When I felt that the women's peace group was in a state of disintegration, all I could do was to tell myself to let go of this way of expressing the Spirit and try to trust that another expression of it would bubble up in another place.

Ritual

A group of young people held a Quaker gathering in York. It was high summer, and half-way through one afternoon they were fed up with being serious so they went out to be tourists. Up Stonegate and down the Shambles, round the medieval city walls they went, in gangs that separated and merged and separated again. They wore T-shirts and shorts or dungarees, and Doc Martens with multi-coloured laces if their feet weren't bare; they sang and fooled about, and people probably thought they were students from Spain or Italy on an intensive language course let out to play. Eventually they converged on the focal point of York, which is the thirteenth-century Minster. Outside the west end of the Minster there is a wide cobbled space, and when they reached it the group suddenly decided, on someone's suggestion reinforced by habit and instinct, to sit down in a circle for a silent Quaker meeting for worship. They sat, heads bowed, saying nothing: a small hollow of quiet in the noise of the city. The tourists and residents of York would now have taken them to be an esoteric cult. After about fifteen minutes they took hands, held for a moment, and then stood up to wander slouching back to base.

It was unplanned, spontaneous, it happened in their free time, yet it proved to be the highlight of their otherwise highly planned weekend. It could be described as a ritual.

Individual lives and communal lives are filled with ritual. There are rituals of getting up and going to bed, of shopping, of Saturday football matches and Sunday church, of union meetings and management seminars, of birthdays and Christmas and summer holidays, of induction into the armed services or a society or club, of national remembrances and religious holy days.

It has come home to me as I've written about my spiritual journey how much I need, as well as freedom for my inner journeyings, some form of ritual. Yet little significant ritual has seemed available for me to mark out the pathways and transitions of my life. The Christian rites and liturgy that I grew up with became an outward form only, evoking in me no spontaneous or natural response. Even my confirmation in the Church of England was uplifting only for a very short time. So I chose to belong to a religious group that abandons all ritual beyond the simplest form. 'In many people's minds,' writes Tom Driver, 'a ritual is . . . what one is obligated to do, not what one feels like doing.'[2] That was how it seemed to me.

The most potent moments that need a public marking are commitment to partnership, birth, and death. I chose the freedom of a Quaker marriage ceremony because I wanted to take my vows spontaneously and I wanted people to say from the heart, in their own words, what they felt about our marriage. When my children were born I couldn't have contemplated asking that they 'fight valiantly under the banner of Christ against sin, the world, and the devil, and continue his faithful soldier and servant to the end of [their] lives'.[3] These were not my words, that was not my way. When people I love have died, I've looked for some expression of loss and grief that is special to that person, rather than a ceremony that repeats the same words in the same order, however beautiful and evocative those words may be.

Ritual, for me, was a prison rather than a pathway. The stillness of the silent meeting, in contrast, offers me gardens – whole landscapes – of inner freedom. Certainly it would be possible for me to sit silently for an hour on my own at home, but the fact that I'm present with other people who are also silent and still confirms my presence in that great landscape. This in itself is a kind of ritual.

Humankind's impulse to enact ritual shows the need to take notice of, make physical recognition of, a time of transition – and to do it not only inwardly and personally, but outwardly with the members of a group; to be consciously, visibly present in that moment of marking, and to use the moment and the presence to move forward into a new form of life. Ritual moments can be informal. They can be meals, like the communion meal we ate at the Mission in Edinburgh, or parties, or circle-dancing, or moments of welcome or farewell. Or they can be formalised. Formality seems especially important at those three key points in our lives.

Partnership, and the transition of birth

Scene: a couple lying in bed. They've been living together for a few years and have just made love. 'This is great,' they say to each other. 'It's too good to keep to ourselves. Let's celebrate – throw a party.' They sit up, grab pens and paper and make lists of who to invite. They pause. 'But how will our friends know,' says one, 'that this is a party specially to celebrate us being *us*? At some point we'll have to call for hush and make an announcement.' 'Yes, we can say something like "We've asked you all here to celebrate the two of us deciding we're going to stay together for good".' They grab another piece of paper and scribble down the things they might say.

It takes them some time to realise that what they're devising is a wedding.

Scene: a garden. People have brought flowers and presents to give to one couple. They all know that this is a wedding but no one quite knows what's going to happen. First they bring out food and drink, get to know each other and talk. Informally, the leader asks people who have come as couples to tell their experience of partnership and commitment, and people who have come alone to talk, perhaps painfully, about their experience of partings and aloneness. Then the couple tell their story: how they met and got to know one another, how they made their decision to marry, what their hopes are for the partnership, and what they're looking for in this ceremony. When the talking is done the leader asks the couple to go away for a time, so that their friends can devise a ritual. Perhaps this is a time for sleep, when the pair sleep separately.

The group choose a moment for the couple to be brought back. When they return, the pair talk about their hopes and fears for the marriage. Others tell of their hopes and fears too, and gradually the ceremony takes on formality. In due course a ritual is enacted and the two spontaneously make their vows: a ritual that is not only what they want, but one that is a surprise to them as well. The element of surprise makes everyone live in the moment, and the element of choice makes the ceremony special to this occasion. The ritual gives way to feasting and dancing, and goes on through the night and into another day.

I remember my own wedding only vaguely. I can remember waking early and wishing we'd arranged the ceremony for eight o'clock in the morning rather than two in the afternoon, and I remember smiling for the cameras till my jaw ached and eating nothing at the reception but the strawberry off the top of the trifle. But my main thought was for the moment when the two of us could drive off alone together at the end.

There are enormous problems with rituals for partnership now in the fragmented societies of the West. More and more couples are setting up their partnerships informally with no public ceremony to mark the event. In earlier centuries, the ritual of marriage made a statement to society: it declared that the individual had left their first family and instituted a new one. Now partnerships and marriages often break up and are re-formed, with the children living with one or other parent in the new situation. A woman can bear a child and bring it up on her own, and gay couples create ceremonies to celebrate their commitment to each other. If a heterosexual pair do decide on a traditional wedding the marriage ceremony in the parish church can be merely an occasion for show, arranged more for the benefit of the video camera than for the edification of the couple or the guests.

What rituals might be devised to match the reality of each person's specific needs, as well as the need of the community to understand and absorb each new situation?

We've assumed in the West that partnership is a matter of individual choice motivated by deep inner feelings of commitment to the other person. In other words, you fall in love and you get together. That's all there is to it. But, as the wrestling of the Quakers over the breaking of one partnership and the formation of another showed, the making or breaking of a partnership involves a significant transition for the community as well as for the two people involved.

In the past, rituals have been prescribed by the community for the individual. Now individuals want to make their own decisions. We want to decide on our own, too, when to bear and how to rear our children. But decisions about children have consequences far beyond what the parents can imagine, and consequences for the community in which they live.

I've described earlier the significance of the births of my children. The particular significance came as a surprise to me, and this may be why it was at this point that I felt most acutely the lack not so much of a celebration of the baby's arrival, which was available to us, but of a marked pathway for the transition into parenthood. I couldn't see, mirrored in the community round me, a recognition of the enormous change that had taken place: the change in us from being free, non-responsible agents to being absolutely responsible for this fragile being at her most vulnerable and formative time.

I remember standing at a Christmas carol service beside a young woman and noticing that she wasn't singing the carols. I wondered if she didn't know the words, but when all the children rejoined their parents her little girl came to stand beside her and sang with the rest of us. The two of us talked over coffee and mince pies afterwards and I found she was speechless with anger. 'Easy, isn't it,' she said, 'to celebrate a baby born two thousand years ago. So easy, and so hypocritical. Would we have celebrated if we'd been there then? Who was around to celebrate the birth of *my* baby?'

She was single; she'd been offered an abortion but decided to have the baby because she wanted to, and because she knew she could love it. But what she'd experienced from her community was cold-shouldering, homelessness and poverty. The friends who had given her real support were those who'd also found mainstream society turning its back on them, including Christians. Yet every year the major ritual of Christianity celebrates the birth of a baby just as despised as this woman's.

Why is there such a lack of rituals to mark the passage into parenthood? There is baptism or christening, but this gives a welcome for the baby not into the community but into a closed religious group. The lack may exist because marriage has traditionally been the immediate precursor of the arrival of children. Now that the commitment to partnership and the birth of children have become so separated, maybe it's time for us to recognise the separate significance of these events both to the individual and to those around them, and mark their signficance in a way that has meaning and depth.

Death and its rituals

I was one of a group of writers who were shocked by the death of one of their number in a car crash. I asked one of the others how he felt about coming to the funeral, because I knew he didn't believe in God. 'It's *because* I don't believe in God that I have come,' he said. 'If God's not there to do it for us, we've got to do it for each other.'

When my friend Jennifer died her three adult children asked Patricia, a Catholic, and me, a Quaker, to come round and plan her funeral. They wanted the twenty minutes at the crematorium to be entirely for Jennifer, and non-religious. We didn't ask ourselves whether the crematorium staff would co-operate with our plans, but in fact they took our instructions and followed them not only to the letter but in spirit too. In preparation we looked at Jennifer's favourite books and read some of the letters she'd shared with us, especially the ones from a friend who sent her hilarious cuttings from the local press. We combed her philosophy textbooks for pieces that had influenced her thinking, and listened to her tapes. In the end we'd collected twenty minutes' worth of remembrance and celebration of Jennifer. As Patricia and I walked into the crematorium her favourite Mozart was playing, and a member of the staff came towards us carrying away the crucifix, murmuring, 'I thought you'd prefer this not to be in view.'

When everyone was in their seats Patricia and I started to read the extracts. Several of them were funny, like Bertrand Russell querying whether the cat who'd crossed the room while you weren't looking was, philosophically speaking, the same cat or a different one from the one who'd been sleeping in the same room a few moments before. It took a while for people to realise that they could laugh. It seemed all right to be grieved at the same time as to laugh, and we felt the real presence of Jennifer in the crematorium, and at the party afterwards when all her friends and family were there and the only person missing was Jennifer.

This rite of passage, for us and for Jennifer, seemed to combine both the elements I'd been looking for: freedom of choice on the one hand and a structured framework on the other. When someone close to me has died and I've been unable or unwilling to expose myself to the trauma of a bare, unfeeling service of cremation or burial, I've felt that an ultimately significant moment has been left unmarked. Death is now mostly hidden from us, and we from it. Funerals like that of my parents, in the parish church where they prayed and sang, are rare. At some funerals, especially in a crematorium, I feel the impulse to wail out loud, like groups of Jewish women do as paid mourners, and then to leave ritual offerings of food reverently at the door of the bereaved person as a way of enabling them to concentrate solely on their grief.

It came to me that I hadn't been able to grieve for my mother, for her death but also for her life, for its limitations, and particularly for the limited and painful relationship I'd had with her. Though she had in the real meaning of the words 'passed on' – though I knew she was in another place, beyond the constraints of body, mind and feeling that had made her life, and my life with her, so difficult – part of her was still locked up in me. It was that part I needed to find, and to bury or cast away.

I resisted the thought for some time. In fact I scarcely articulated it in this form. Eventually I found a counsellor trained in psychosynthesis, a discipline which emphasises the importance of ritual as a way of moving forward in the psyche and in the soul. After several sessions of getting to the core of my feelings she suggested that I should bring to her house, high up in the Welsh hills, some

133

things of my mother's. I brought flowers, papers, odd items that I'd kept for no special reason. She invited me to do whatever I wanted to do with each of them, and I did, honouring them and cursing them with no logic, just letting everything that was in me flow out, pleasing myself and shocking myself by turns.

I was sitting on a slate window seat where there was some attractive pottery and a candle or two and some matches. By instinct, without consciously thinking, I knew I wanted to burn some of my mother's things. I took a match and lit the candle and used it to set them alight. Then I screamed – 'What shall I do with these flaming sheets of paper?' and I dropped them in one of the pots, more to save them from falling on the carpet and setting fire to the house than from any deep psychological motive.

Now that I'd found a safe way of doing it I burned more and more, slowly and meditatively. When I'd finished, I gazed at the pot as the smoke from the burned papers rose out of it, and it was an urn. It was my mother's urn; it contained her ashes. I felt reverent towards the urn and its contents, with no anger, but real grief. I wanted to treat the ashes with absolute respect as the remnant of my mother on earth.

I asked if I could have a smaller urn and transfer the ashes to it. I wanted to carry it to somewhere I could scatter them. I already knew where would be the right place. With the slowness of meditation I carried the little urn to the car and drove gently down the hill to the river in the valley, which was fast flowing and rocky. I stood on the bridge. When there was no one in sight I tipped the ashes in little jerks over into the water. My mother loved mountain rivers, so I knew this was an ending she would enjoy. Some of the ashes fell on mossy rocks, some were carried away in the stream.

I was the doer and also the observer of what I did. It was a ritual observance, offered to me by someone who knew the power of ritual to transform: again, in the literal sense, to trans-form, to change my form of thinking, of being, from one that was locked in the past into one that could move into the future. Though it was private, intensely personal to me and my situation, I think I could have welcomed some more public ritual if it was in the spirit of the specific as well as the common situation.

How can we respond to the tension between the need both for public recognition of a changed situation and for uniqueness and spontaneity? I would like to be open to new forms of ritual: perhaps adaptations of the old forms, like Jennifer's funeral; or new ways, like the wedding in the garden; or new concepts altogether. We could welcome a baby not solely into a church but into the non-sectarian community, and combine it with a commitment to support the parents in bringing up their child. With the making of a partnership, a couple who don't choose to marry legally but simply want to commit themselves to each other could arrange a celebration to do just that.

An era of rapid change lends itself to changing responses. Maybe we can surprise ourselves by being creative in new and different ways. Maybe we can develop the kind of spiritual literacy which finds new forms to go with the new words.

Tension and paradox

> Listen, Pilgrim! There are no roads.
> Roads are made by walking.
> Listen, Pilgrim – there are no books.
> Books are made by writing.
> Listen, Pilgrim: there are no words.
> Words are made by speaking,
> words are made by listening,
> by hearing and being heard.

Of course there are roads, books, words. But they take on reality when we find them for ourselves. The spiritual journey is made by travelling. The words for it are made by communicating our experiences as we go.

I hold in my mind two paradoxical insights, one that was part of a conversation at a party, the other that was spoken ministry in a Quaker meeting for worship. 'Two things are essential: to recognise that the world is a terrible place and to try to change it, and at the same time to accept things absolutely and lovingly as they are.' And: 'Two things are essential: firstly to hold to our truth as we've experienced it, and secondly to think it possible that we may be mistaken.'

In the spiritual life, the central paradox is that we need to be alone and we need to be together. None of us can exist on our own. We are defined as human beings by living together. Each unique individual is born into the community on which they are dependent, and which is changed by the coming of each new member. But if the identity or the image of the community is more important than the identity of the individual – if the individual is crushed or silenced – the purpose of the community itself is negated.

John Berger says of the doctor whom he calls *A Fortunate Man*: 'He tries to keep the personality company in its loneliness.'[4] The human condition is essentially lonely. Each of us is born alone and will die alone. None of us can live another's life for them, or have our lives lived except by ourselves. Yet we need company in our loneliness; we need listening to, we need recognition and love.

The tension between the individual and the community is the central thread of all philosophy, psychology and social science. There is only one substance, interwoven with this thread, that can make the tension creative instead of destructive. That is the spiritual substance of love: a love that stretches out from a fundamental respect for itself towards a fundamental respect for the other. 'Love,' wrote Erich Fromm, 'is only possible if [people] communicate with each other from the centre of their existence . . . Love is not a resting place, but a moving, growing, working together; even whether there is harmony or conflict, joy or sadness, is secondary to the fundamental fact that . . . people experience themselves from the essence of their existence, that they are one with each other by being one with themselves.'[5]

We can only be one with each other by each being one with our own being.

Sometimes I challenge my idiosyncratic use of language with a sentence beginning, 'In the end, there's only . . .' and ask how I, now, can complete it.

At the moment, this is how it goes:

'In the end, there is only the respect I have for myself, and a willingness to open that self to others, and be open to the selves that others reveal to me.'

Or, to put it another way:

'In the end, there is only the courage to be what we are. And then to live what we are, not in opposition to but together with each other.'

POSTSCRIPT

❧ *Entering my journey, offering our stories* ❧

I am the bride, I sang: and I am the bridegroom.
I am shameless, she sang: and I am ashamed.
I am an alien, I sang: and I am a citizen.
Hear of me in gentleness, she sang: and learn of me
in roughness.
I am, I sang: the knowledge of my name.
I am the first, we sang together: and I am the last.
(MICHÈLE ROBERTS, *The Wild Girl*[1])

Alone

I am inside my mind. I am a river. No, I am a lake, a small round tarn high in the mountains. Trickles of water ease through moss and peat and form themselves into streams that push between boulders, seep along reedy flatnesses and throw themselves over the edge of cliffs. I am the moss, I am the boulders, I am the reed and the cliff. I am the single thorn bush on the shore. But most of all I am the water, from the moment when it condenses in the air and becomes falling rain to the moment when it is absorbed as nourishment into the root of the plant.

I am the stream, and I am the lake. I am the steep crags round the lake that throw deep shadows over it and shelter it from fierce winds.

I am the wind. I drive rocks before me, carrying them, throwing them blindly into the paths of fleeing animals. I root up great trees and hurl them. I destroy. I am driven by fiercer winds behind me, destroying. I heave wild waves up from the lake, then drop them back in torment. Then I let go, and soften, and am still.

I hold still in my grief, hold my grief in stillness. The

137

pattern of destruction lies lightly on my surface as if it were meant to be there. Deep down below, in the lake, lie the ends of things, immovable. Nothing moves the death that lies heavy within me. It is the base of all things, it carries the weight of all things. There is nothing for it but to be. It hides from the moon, it hides from the sun. But it is there.

Over and above, round and through, I am the sun that moves each day from one side to the other and disappears into the black of the night. I am the moon that reflects a sliver of an orb in the deep of the water. I am the water that flows on down the mountain, over the plain and into the salt sea.

The picture changes. I am colour. Here is an art gallery, and people are flocking in to see the paintings. The people are small, the paintings are big. No – there is one painting only, which covers every wall, even the ceiling of the gallery, even its floor. The people are overwhelmed by it, they crick their necks gazing at the ceiling and hover close to each wall to absorb the vivid, seething brightness. Every colour they ever knew is there, and colours they have never seen before. I am one of the visitors overwhelmed by the colour. I am wrapped around by it. Then I am the colour itself. The colour is a song I am singing, a song that I am.

Now the ceiling of the gallery rises, and lightens, and becomes a clear glass dome looking out to the sky. The colour still covers the walls, but now the walls stretch out, every angle disappearing until the room is perfectly round.

The people are singing like I was singing, and they hold scarves of all the many colours. They are dancing with the scarves. No, they're skating, and the coloured floor now falls into a bowl in the same way that the ceiling rose into a dome, and the people are skate-boarding over the bowl, waving their coloured scarves round their heads and singing. Everything is movement and colour and sound. They whirl and become one.

I am one of the people, I am all the different people. I am all the colours, and I am the song.

Together

Two women are talking. One has lost her mother through death, the other has recently had a baby.

A: No one believed me. They all said, 'You know Mum, she's always fought things, she'll come through this.' But I saw what she looked like, I knew she was dying. You remember how we fought, how lonely I felt because she didn't seem to love me, how angry I got because she couldn't accept me for what I was, she always seemed to wish I was different? That was because I spotted her rebellious side, I knew she wasn't all quiet and demure, I knew she was just as rebellious as me inside, only she'd never dared show it. So I saw her how no one else saw her.

B: I used to think you were wicked, the way you talked about your mother. To me she was the incarnation of sweetness, the model for us all.

A: We didn't say goodbye. I said I'd come back next day. I could have said, 'You're dying, aren't you, Mum? Do you want to say goodbye?' But I wasn't sure that I could say that.

B: Sure that she was dying, or sure that she knew?

A: Sure that she knew. But I knew. I went home – it was about eleven o'clock – and went to bed. No one else was there, they'd gone off on holiday to their Gran's. I suppose I must have slept a bit because the next I knew it was two in the morning. I lay quite still, with my eyes wide open. It was dark, and I was just waiting.

B: Waiting? What for?

A: Nothing. Just waiting. Then a bright light filled the whole room, and I knew it was Jesus.

B: Jesus?

A: Yes.

B: (*betrayed by the change in her friend*) But you're not a Christian!

A: It makes no difference. That's what I saw.

(They are uncomfortable. They go out for a walk, come back and sit over cups of tea to shake off their discomfort.)

B: *(with effort)* Go on. Tell me about the bright light and Jesus.

A: The light was strongest at the end of the bed. There wasn't a figure standing there or anything, just – light. I knew it was Jesus. And something said . . .

B: Jesus spoke? You heard words?

A: Stop being so literal! They were sort of words and not-words. It was like knowing, in my head. Only it came in words from the light at the end of the bed.

B: What did the words say?

A: They said, 'It's all right. I'm taking her with me.'

B: *It's* all right, or *she's* all right?

A: I don't know. One or the other. Both. It's the same, anyway. I knew she'd died, and I knew she was all right.

B: And she had died.

A: Yes. I phoned the hospital and they said she'd died then, just when I saw Jesus.

B: You must have been shattered.

A: I wasn't shattered one bit. I knew even though I'd lost her she'd be fine. I was shattered later – I'm shattered now – but I still know she's fine.

B: How can you *know?* How can you be sure you're not just reassuring yourself?

A: I can't explain. I just know.

B: You can't be sure.

A: Yes, I can.

B: How? *(part envious, part angry with her friend for this madness)* I don't believe in that kind of knowing.

A: Go on. You know things. Tell me what you know.

B: I know that everything's different for me now James has come. I know I love him. It's so big, how I love him. I've never felt anything as powerful. I know I could never not love him. Do you know that it's all right for your mum like I know about loving James?

A: Something like that.

(*Silence. They both know that A is estranged from her teenage daughter*)

A: Do you have visions? Like – oh, I don't know – that you and James once met in a previous incarnation or something?

B: No, no, we come from different planets. He's a complete stranger. It's my job to get to know him. That's what makes it so wonderful. I thought a baby of mine would be like me and that's why I'd love them. But he's different and I still love him. It's a miracle.

A: Aren't you frightened?

B: Why should I be?

A: That things will change.

B: (*realising that A is hurt*) I'm frightened I won't be up to it. That the practical things – the lack of sleep, needing more money, mopping up sick, dragging baby-buggies and baby-bags everywhere – that it'll all get me down and I won't cope. (*She notices that C, the baby's father, has come in*) That *we* won't cope.

C: Frightened? Sure I'm frightened. It's all happened so quickly. One day there's just us, next day there's this wonderful tiny thing who can't do anything, even live, without us. I'm scared witless.

A: And she's got all the clinics, all the other mums to turn to. You haven't.

C: I don't want to do it alone, I want to share it – not only the chores, the responsibility, but how fantastic it is, how James is a new person in the world and no one knows what he's going to be, how he's going to develop and turn out,

141

how everything that happens to him will go to make up this unique person, what difference it'll make to the world now he's here.

B: Yes. He's ours, but he's everyone else's too.

A: Maybe if, out there, they had some way of saying that – of saying how great it was that this new baby had arrived, and that they'd take some of the load off you, it'd make all the difference . . . I know something. It'd have made all the difference to me.

(James cries, and A cries too)

The pattern

The air is full of seagulls. They're flying at random, though in roughly the same direction. They must have taken flight together at the same moment but in no sense are they flying together.

Then, as I watch, their separate flights take on pattern and shape. One mass shapes into a line, others into the classic beauty of the V. As they have flown from one side of my horizon to the other, their mass has changed from muddle to order, from insignificance to significance.

How do they know that they must do it, and how they must do it? How does a separate bird, with its own instinct and mind-set, decide to follow this bird in front to the left rather than that bird in front to the right? What pecking order or currents of air are guiding the movement of each wing? One thing is certain: there isn't time for each to think about it, to ponder the feathers as they lift and swerve and to decide by will and calculation to follow in the right way. It is the product of evolution and instinct, individual stamina, discipline, and sensitivity to pattern.

Nor do they know that they are beautiful. What is it about the pattern that comes to my perception as beauty?

The circle

A people gather round a fire as the sun goes down. Old and young are there, women and men, the lame and the runner, the ones who have been present at these occasions countless times and the ones for whom it is the first time ever. They sit and crouch, kneel or slouch, cuddle into the arms of someone big and safe, sit slightly apart or in a group of family or close friends.

Silence falls. There are leaders, those with long experience whom people admire. They start to talk. Not to address the assembled crowd, not to introduce other speakers, but simply to start things off. 'The cost of everything!' they say. 'Isn't it terrible? How it goes up and up!' Mutters run round the people. 'Dreadful. Everyone's felt it. . . .' Someone pipes up with a particularly appalling instance. The rest murmur shock and sympathy.

Then: 'My grandmother used to say, about the cost of everything. . . .'

Ah – everyone knows this grandmother. Or knew. For when asked, 'How is your grandmother?' the speaker has to say sadly that within the last year she has died.

'What a woman!' goes up the cry. 'You remember how she used to talk?'

And stories are told about the grandmother. Arguments break out about different views of her character and talents and are resolved with a laugh or a disgruntled, 'Well, *I* knew her *best*.' She was like that one's old father, just the opposite of this one's grandmother. Her story leads on: how can the character of someone old be so different from their character when young, or stay so much the same? What is the nature of age? Does it always bring wisdom? What is wisdom?

'That woman,' says one, eventually. 'She was like the old woman they used to talk about who wandered through the village one day in search of her lost chickens. . . .'

Only one or two people remember this tale, so the speaker has to tell it right from the beginning through to the end.

So, as the night deepens and more wood is heaped on the great fire in the centre of the circle, the gathered people becomes a people of story-telling. No one knows which story might be told next, or whether the story is true, or whether it started true and became embroidered in the telling, or if it came direct from the speaker's imagination or has been handed down through generation upon generation. Some tales have changed so much in the many tellings that it would be unrecognisable to the person who started it off.

Back and back the stories go, until they start to encompass the history of the people. Stories are told of the growth and conflicts and splits and reshapings of the whole people and their land. The land is crucial to them, and the stories go on to tell about the land: how the rivers flooded one year and sank into drought the next, how the mountains eroded or exploded, how crops failed or grew, how the cattle thrived or roamed or were raided by the people from the next tract of land; how homes were built, then destroyed by fire or taken over by new owners and changed, decorated or rebuilt. They remember quarrels, fierce battles, wounds, healing, death and reconciliations.

Everyone has a chance to speak, whether to add to the story, to ask questions about it or decide it's the end of that one and start another one fresh.

Gradually, the stories slow in pace. The tone changes: not so much 'Have you heard about the way that. . . .?' as '. . . Is it possible that it might have. . . .?' The stories begin to take on magic. How dragons came out of the mountain . . . how the lost child spoke in the voice of truth from out of the thorn tree . . . how the monster from the south had the head of a dragon and the heart of a man. How giants made thunder – how demons made earthquakes – how the gods came to earth and abandoned it again. How dreams told when crops would grow or fail. How time comes round again, or years vanish, or spirits return in other forms. How we choose where to be born. How we know when we will die.

The people are entering a place of doubt and hope and mystery. Look at the logs on the fire. How did wood begin? And fire, and light? Look at the sparks rising up into the sky – they are like stars. Why are the stars up there? Do they ever fall to earth? What do stars mean to people, and what do people mean to the stars? How did it all begin?

As the stars move slowly overhead, people drift into sleep and wake again. They bring food to sustain themselves through the night and share it round the circle. They reprove quarrellers and interrupters and are reproved themselves in turn.

Darkness begins to lift, and the sky turns to that strange point of dawn when it is both deep and pale. A voice begins to speak about the creation of the world.

Others speak, offering their stories about the beginnings of life. Now no one contradicts or argues. They simply leave what is said lying in the circle in front of the dying fire. The beginning of the world, the beginning of life, the beginning of soul: it is the story of all things, the story of what no one can know and what everyone knows.

Many of them are asleep now, and more fall asleep as the dawn grows. The words fall gently on them like patches for a cloak. Some of the words will be remembered, many will be forgotten; some will be repeated next year and the next and the next. It doesn't matter. It is the occasion that matters, the coming together, the fire, the circle, the listening and the talk. It is life, it is renewal and letting go. It will happen again, and in the times between, the stories take a place deep inside the people, outwardly forgotten but woven into the fabric of their lives. Without the stories they would be naked and cold. Sometimes, when they remember the night of story-telling, they smile and feel energy flowing into themselves for the day's tasks. They need stories like they need each other. They need to know, and speculate, to wonder and forget and remember. They need the fire and the circle and the stories. They need the word, the many words, and they need the silence. They go beyond the silence into sleep.

REFERENCES

1: Introduction

1. Thomas Merton, *Thirty Poems*, New Directions, 1944. Quoted in Monica Furlong, *Thomas Merton*, Collins, 1980.
2. George Fox, *Journal*, revised edition by John L. Nickalls, Religious Society of Friends, 1975.
3. Charles Morgan, *The Voyage*, Macmillan, 1941, p. 227, out of print.
4. George Eliot, *Middlemarch*, Penguin edition, 1965, p. 243.
5. *Advices and Queries*, 1995, number 1, Religious Society of Friends, London NW1 2BJ.
6. Canon W. H. Vanstone, *Love's Endeavour, Love's Expense*, Darton, Longman & Todd, 1977, p. 5.
7. Joanna Field (Marion Milner), *A Life of One's Own*, Virago, 1986, p. 87.
8. Janet Frame, *To the Is-land*, Grafton Books, 1987.
9. John Berger and Jean Mohr, *A Fortunate Man*, Allen Lane, The Penguin Press, 1967.

2: Let me be warmed

1. Unpublished poem, 'First Stirrings'.
2. Lewis Carroll, *Alice's Adventures In Wonderland*, Chapter Two.
3. A. A. Milne, *The House at Pooh Corner*, Chapter Ten.
4. Edmund Gosse, *Father and Son*, Penguin, 1983, p. 56.
5. Methodist Hymn Book, *circa* 1952.
6. Sheila Rowbotham, in *Truth, Dare or Promise*, ed. Liz Heron, Virago, 1985, p. 200.
7. Alison Leonard, *An Inch of Candle*, Angus & Robertson, 1980, Fontana, 1982, out of print.

3: The girl in the bathroom singing

1. Penelope Farmer, *Eve, Her Story*, Abacus, 1986, pp. 184–5.
2. Toni Morrison, *The Bluest Eye*, Picador, 1990, pp. 88–9.

3. Letter from Anne Wade to the author.
4. Brian Patten, 'Ode on Celestial Music', in *The Oxford Book of Twentieth Century English Verse*, Oxford University Press, 1973.
5. Virginia Woolf, *To The Lighthouse*, Penguin, 1964, pp. 57–8.
6. Iris Murdoch, *The Black Prince*, Penguin, 1975, pp. 316–17.
7. Sheila Rowbotham, quoted by Sara Maitland, lecture on Theology and Art, 17 January 1994.

4: Discovering my own heartbeat

1. Quoted by Fiona McCarthy in her biography of Eric Gill, Faber, 1989.
2. Simone Weil, *Waiting for God*. Copyright 1951 C. P. Putnam's.
3. Toni Morrison, *Beloved*, Chatto & Windus, 1987, p. 141.
4. G. Bernard Shaw, 'St Joan', in *The Complete Plays*, Hamlyn, 1965, p. 1000.
5. H. A. Williams, *The True Wilderness*, Constable, 1965, reissued by Mowbray, Morehouse Publishing, 1994.

Interval: Meditation on a Meditation

1. A Buddhist concept: 'enigmatic challenges or quests guaranteed to lead you into places beyond your imagining' (Rose Flint).

5: Drawing a profile for that which has no form

1. From *Available Light*, Alfred A. Knopf, New York, 1988.
2. In *SHE*, July 1987.
3. Published in *Quaker Monthly*, July 1980. QHS, Friends House, London NW1 2BJ.
4. 'you fell asleep drinking', by Alta, published by Shameless Hussy Press, Berkeley CA, USA and in *In The Pink*, The Women's Press, 1983.
5. Leo Tolstoy, *Resurrection*, Penguin, 1966, p. 561.
6. Jackie Kohnstamm, 'The Secret of the Lake', in *Brought to Book*, HarperCollins, 1994.
7. See Chapter 1, p. 8.

6: First and last mysteries

1. Published in *Sex and God*, ed. Linda Hurcombe, Routledge & Kegan Paul, 1987.
2. *Collins English Dictionary*, 1986.

3. Daphne Hampson, *Theology and Feminism*, Blackwell, 1990.
4. *Advices and Queries*, number 7, op. cit. NW1 2BJ.
5. *Living the Questions*, ed. Edward Robinson. Religious Experience Research Unit, Oxford, 1978.
6. Jane Sherwood, *Post Mortem Journal*, Spearman, 1967.
7. Rose Tremain, in Claire Boylan (ed.), *The Agony and the Ego*, Penguin, 1993.
8. John Donne, 'The Exstasie', from *The Metaphysical Poets*, Oxford University Press, 1921.
9. Donne, 'Hymn to God the Father', ibid.
10. D. H. Lawrence, 'We are transmitters – ', in *Selected Poems*, Penguin, 1950.
11. BBC Radio 4, May 1992 and May 1994.
12. Berger and Mohr, op. cit.
13. Dervla Murphy, *Wheels Within Wheels*, Penguin, 1981, p. 187.
14. In The Boston Women's Collective, *Our Bodies Ourselves*, UK edition, Penguin, 1979, p. 84.
15. Ann Oakley, *Taking It Like A Woman*, Flamingo, 1985, pp. 184–5.
16. Eliot, op. cit., pp. 844–5.

Interval: On shadows

1. Thomas Keneally, *Schindler's Ark*, Hodder & Stoughton, 1982.
2. William Shakespeare, *King Lear*, Act III, Scene VII.
3. Laurens van der Post, *Jung and the Story of Our Time*, Hogarth Press, 1976.
4. George Fox, *Journal*, ed. Nickalls, entry for 1647.
5. Brian Keenan, *An Evil Cradling*, Vintage, 1992.
6. W. B. Yeats, 'Easter 1916'.
7. *Clarissa and the Nasties*, short story in *Writing Women*, Vol. 5, No. 3.
8. C. P. Taylor, *Good*, Methuen, 1982.
9. Quoted in Don Cupitt, *The Sea of Faith*, BBC, 1984.
10. 'Face to Faith', *The Guardian*, June 1989.
11. Nag Hammadi Library 126.

7: Healings and leadings

1. Joanna Rogers Macy, *Despair and Power in the Nuclear Age*, New Society Publishers, Philadelphia, USA, 1983.
2. Don Cupitt, *Taking Leave of God*, SCM Press, 1980.
3. Val Smith's account is published in *Through The Looking Glass, Portrait of a Disabled Writers' Group*, Cheshire County Council, 1993.

4. Nadezhda Mandelstam, *Hope against Hope*, Collins, 1971.
5. Paul Tillich, *The Shaking of the Foundations*, Scribners, 1948.
6. In *Available Light*, Alfred Knopf, New York, 1988.
7. Roger Fisher and William Ury, *Getting to Yes*, Hutchinson Business, 1986.

8: Transforming me into us

1. Referring to a ritual at times of crisis performed by the Mbuti of Zaire. Quoted in Tom F. Driver, *The Magic of Ritual*, p. 153, published by HarperSanFrancisco, 1991.
2. Ibid.
3. *The Alternative Service Book* of the Church of England, 1980. SPCK, Cambridge University Press, Hodder & Stoughton, Oxford University Press.
4. Berger and Mohr, op. cit.
5. Erich Fromm, *The Art of Loving*, Allen & Unwin, 1975.

Postscript: Entering my journey, offering our stories

1. Gnostic text, 'Thunder Perfect Mind', quoted in Michèle Roberts, *The Wild Girl*, Minerva, 1983.

INDEX

Advices and Queries (Quaker) 9, 87

Alta 79

Alternative Service Book, The (Church of England) 45, 128

Aquinas, Thomas 63

Augustine, St 63

Bach, J. S. 24

Baha'i faith 9, 48–50, 60, 76

Beatles, the 54

Benner, Joan 79

Bennett, Alan 74, 90

Berger, John 13, 97, 136

birth 78–80, 131–2

Blyton, Enid 54

Boston Women's Collective, the 98

Brady, Ian 103

Brontë, Emily 8

Bunyan, John 32–4

cancer 4, 7

Carroll, Lewis 17

Catholicism 9

cerebral palsy 113

Chagall, Marc 59

Chekhov, Anton 15

Cheshire, Leonard 47

Christian Union 3, 42, 44–6

class system, British 39–40, 51, 55

clearness groups 125–6

communion 32, 41, 46, 79, 129

confirmation 24–6

Creation Spirituality 10

creative listening 121, 126–7

creed 5–9, 23, 24, 62, 73

Cuba crisis 47, 116

Cupitt, Don 112

Darwin, Charles 44

Dead Sea Scrolls 59

death 80–1, 132–5

diary-writing 4–5, 11–13

discernment, meetings for 126

Donne, John 94–5

Driver, Tom 128

el Saadawi, Nawal 94

Eliot, George 8, 15, 82, 101

existentialism 86

Farmer, Penelope 38

Faulkner, Anthony 94

Field, Joanna (Marion Milner) 11

Fisher, Roger 122

151

Flint, Rose 147
Forster, E. M. 9
Fox, George 2, 31, 32, 104
Fox, Matthew 10
Frame, Janet 11
Freeman, John 57
Fromm, Erich 136

Gandhi, Mahatma 117
Genet, Jean 42
Gill, Eric 51
Golding, William 126
Gosse, Edmund 18
Griffin, Susan 85
guru 57

Hampson, Daphne 86
Heidegger, Martin 81
Hindley, Myra 106
Hitler, Adolf 106
Hunt, Leigh 36
Hymn Book, Methodist 19
hymns 19, 34

Icke, David 32
Islam 9, 59

James, William 88
Jenkins, David 19
Jewish faith 9, 58–60
Joan, St 64
Julian the Apostate 1
Jung, C. G. 57, 104

Keenan, Brian 104
Keneally, Thomas 103
Kennedy, John F. 47
kibbutz 59
Kierkegaard, Søren 63
King, Martin Luther 117
Kohnstamm, Jackie 80–1

Lawrence, D. H. 95–6

Lawrence, T. E. 89

Macleod, Iain 52
Macy, Joanna Rogers 110
Mandelstam, Nadezhda 116
Maxwell, Robert 61
Mead, Margaret 94
Mendelssohn, Felix 31
Merton, Thomas 1
Milne, A. A. 17
Milner, Marion 11
missionaries 27–8
Mohr, Jean 13
Mondrian, Piet 15
Moore, Brian 94
Morgan, Charles 3
Mormons 77, 94
Morrison, Toni 40, 63, 90
Mozart, Wolfgang Amadeus 133
Murdoch, Iris 42
Murphy, Dervla 98

Oakley, Ann 99
O'Malley, Mary 94
Origen 63

Patten, Brian 42
Paul, St 63
peace movement 84, 116–18
peak experiences 88–9
Peter, St 26
philosophy 57, 86, 88
Piercy, Marge 72, 120, 122
Pinter, Harold 15, 42
Profumo affair 47
psychosynthesis 66, 133

reincarnation 8
Rhodes, Neil 102–3, 106
Rhodesia 52–3
Roberts, Michèle 137

Robinson, Edward 88–9
Robinson, John 47–8
Rohr, Richard 1
Rowbotham, Sheila 22, 46
Russell, Bertrand 133

Shakespeare, William 36, 103, 106
Shaw, Bernard 64
Sherwood, Jane 89
Smith, Val 113–14
Stainer, John 24

Taizé 36
Taylor, C. P. 106
Teresa, Mother 106
theology 85–6
Tillich, Paul 119
Tolstoy, Leo 80

Townsend, Sue 9
Tremain, Rose 90–1
Turnbull, Colin 124

Ury, William 122

van der Post, Laurens 104
Vanstone, Canon W. H. 10
Vincent, Ben 6

Wade, Anne 41–2
Weil, Simone 62
Welburn, Vivienne 22
Weldon, Fay 90
Williams, H. A. 65, 100
Wittgenstein, Ludwig 108
Woolf, Virginia 43

Yeats, W. B. 105
yoga 9, 121